WATERFORD

W9-BHZ-204

# Essential
# Ireland

**AAA Publishing** 1000 AAA Drive, Heathrow, Florida 32746

**Ireland:** Regions and Best places to see

★ Best places to see 34–55        ■ Featured sight

The East 81–110        The West 137–158

The South 111–136        The North 159–187

**Original text by Penny Phenix**
Updated by Apostrophe S Limited

American editor: G.K. Sharman

Edited, designed and produced by AA Publishing
© Automobile Association Developments Limited 2007
Maps © Automobile Association Developments Limited 2007

This edition printed 2007, reprinted Oct 2007

ISBN-13: 978-1-59508-177-3
ISBN-10: 1-59508-177-1

Published in the United States by AAA Publishing,
1000 AAA Drive, Heathrow, Florida 32746
Published in the United Kingdom by AA Publishing

Color separation: MRM Graphics Ltd
Printed and bound in Italy by Printer Trento S.r.l.

A03164

This product includes mapping data licensed from Ordnance
Survey of Northern Ireland® reproduced by permission
of the Chief Executive, acting on behalf of the Controller of
Her Majesty's Stationery Office. © Crown Copyright 2007.
Permit number 70125

Republic of Ireland mapping based on Ordnance Survey Ireland. Permit No. 8136
© Ordnance Survey Ireland and Government of Ireland

# About this book

This book is divided into five sections.

**The essence of Ireland** pages 6–19
Introduction; Features; Food and Drink;
Short Break including the 10 Essentials

**Planning** pages 20–33
Before You Go; Getting There; Getting
Around; Being There

**Best places to see** pages 34–55
The unmissable highlights of any visit
to Ireland

**Best things to do** pages 56–77
Good places to have lunch; stunning
scenery; top activities; boat trips; places
to take the children; traditional music
and more

**Exploring** pages 78–187
The best places to visit in Ireland,
organized by area

**Maps** All map references are to the
maps on the covers. For example, Cork
has the reference 🕂 17H – indicating
the grid square in which it can be found.

**Prices** An indication of the cost of
restaurants and cafés at attractions is
given by €/£ signs: €€€/£££ denotes
higher prices, €€/££ denotes average
prices, €/£ denotes lower prices.

**Hotel prices** Room per night (Republic
of Ireland/Northern Ireland): €/£ budget
(under €85/£50); €€/££ moderate
(€85–€150/£50–£90); €€€/£££
expensive to luxury (over €150/£90)

**Restaurant prices** A three-course meal
per person without drinks Republic of
Ireland/Northern Ireland: €/£ budget
(under €20/£12); €€/££ moderate
(€20–€40/£12–£24); €€€/£££ expensive
to luxury (over €40/£24)

# Contents

## THE ESSENCE OF...

6 – 19

## PLANNING

20 – 33

## BEST PLACES TO SEE

34 – 55

**BEST THINGS TO DO**

56 – 77

**EXPLORING...**

78 – 187

# The essence of...

Introduction          8–9

Features             10–11

Food and Drink       12–15

Short Break          16–19

If your time in Ireland is limited you will need to be selective, and one of the best ways of making your selections is by asking the locals. The conversations that will inevitably ensue will be as rewarding as the information you will glean. The essence of Ireland and the friendly good humour of the Irish people are inextricably linked.

Ireland has great cities in each of its four quarters – Dublin in the east, Belfast in the north, Limerick and Galway in the west and Cork in the south – and just a short visit to each will demonstrate the differences in character between these regions.

features

Back in the 1980s, though the scenery was absolutely magical and the hospitality wonderful, there was undercurrent of sadness in Ireland at the ailing economy and the rampant depopulation, particularly among the young. Many properties were being snapped up by outsiders for use as holiday homes, which would stand empty for much of the year.

Visiting the Republic today you will find that the magic in the scenery and the genuinely welcoming people remain unchanged. But where there was concern for the future there is now great optimism. EU membership has turned the economy round, the flow of emigration has reversed and areas that were once down-at-heel are regenerating. Ireland has its own way of combining prosperity and progress with tradition and a relaxed attitude to life.

As of old, nothing is so urgent that it should stand in the way of a good conversation with someone you have only just met. Do not be deterred from visiting Northern Ireland, where the sporadic hostilities are far outweighed by the friendliness of the majority of the population, the beautiful scenery, the interesting historic buildings and many cultural activities.

## GEOGRAPHY

- Ireland lies on the continental shelf to the west of the European mainland. To the east, over the Irish Sea, lies Britain, with Scotland 21km (13 miles) to the northeast.
- In area Ireland is 7 million hectares (17.3 million acres) and of those, around a third are devoted to agriculture.
- The largest county is Cork and the smallest is Louth.
- The highest mountain is Carrantuohill, 1,041m (3,415ft), in the Macgillicuddy's Reeks range of Co Kerry.
- The longest river is the Shannon at 340km (210 miles), while the largest lake is Lough Neagh at 396sq km (153sq miles).
- Ireland has some of Europe's emptiest and cleanest beaches, with great expanses of silvery sands and little rocky coves.
- There are thousands of lakes in Ireland, particularly in the 'lakeland counties', which extend southwards from the border with Northern Ireland, and in Connemara.
- There is a large number of nature reserves all over Ireland that are rich in animal and plant life, and the national parks preserve some large areas of great beauty.

## SPORT AND LEISURE

- Salmon season: January to September.
- Brown trout season: 15 February to 12 October.
- Sea trout fishing: June to September (or 12 October in some places).
- There is no closed season for coarse fishing, and sea angling is possible all year round.
- Ireland has over 11,000 pubs.
- There are over 400 golf courses in Ireland.

food & drink

**Eating out in Ireland is as unhurried an experience as anything else in this relaxing island, and the generally high standard of cooking and service, and the quality of the ingredients, are certainly well worth savouring.**

In all the major towns and cities there is a good variety of food on offer, and traditional Irish cuisine has enjoyed a revival, often with the occasional international influence. Away from the fast-food places, eating out in Ireland is not particularly cheap, but travellers on a budget will find a choice of restaurants throughout the country which offer a 'tourist menu' of good food at reasonable prices.

Specialities to look for include local cheeses, of which there are many, such as the delicious Cashel Blue, Cooleeney, St Killian, Durrus, Chetwynd Blue and Mizen. Irish seafood is also legendary, with fresh lobster, oysters, mussels and scallops.

## IRISH CUISINE

Irish cooking has a reputation for being plain but plentiful, which does it something of a disservice, because the traditional dishes have wonderfully rich flavours and interesting taste combinations.

In recent years dishes that were designed to satisfy the hunger of hard-working farmers and fishermen have been adapted to suit the lesser appetites of those who have done no more than a bit of gentle sightseeing. What was once

dismissed as 'peasant food' has now become a delicacy, such as *drisheen* (black pudding), *cruibeens* (pigs' trotters), Dublin coddle (a sausage stew), beef stewed in Guinness and, of course, Irish stew.

Potato dishes such as *champ* (mashed with chives and butter) or *colcannon* (mashed, mixed with leek, butter, cabbage, cream and nutmeg) are a tasty accompaniment, and adventurous diners can sample edible seaweed in the form of dulce or carrageen pudding.

Irish bread is not just something to make a sandwich with. There are lots of tasty varieties that only need a spreading of butter or a side dish of home-made soup. Soda bread, or wheaten bread, made with stone-ground flour, has a wonderful flavour and texture and there are lots of fruity tea breads such as Barm brack. There is even a potato bread (mashed potato mixed with flour and egg) that is cooked on a griddle and often served with the enormous traditional Irish breakfast of bacon, eggs, sausage and black (or white) pudding.

## WHISKEY AND BEER

Think of Irish beer and it is probably a pint of Guinness that springs to mind. Sold in at least 30 countries world wide, Guinness is a great symbol of Irishness, but undoubtedly tastes best on Irish soil, with its cool, biting taste and thick creamy head. Hard on the heels of Guinness are two other stouts, Beamish and Murphy's, both brewed in Cork, while Smithwicks offers a smooth-tasting bitter which is similar to English beer. Lager is also widely available to those who prefer a more continental taste.

Irish whiskey also has a world market and has a wonderful clean flavour, quite different from Scotch whisky or American bourbon. Four main brands are produced by the Irish Distillers company – Bushmills, Jameson, Powers and Paddy, with pure malts of various ages as well as blended whiskey. The Bushmills Distillery in Northern Ireland and Jameson's at Midleton, Co Cork give guided tours which explain the distilling process.

**short break**

If you have only a short time to visit Ireland and would like to take home some unforgettable memories you can do something local and capture the real flavour of the country. The following suggestions will give you a wide range of sights and experiences that won't take very long, won't cost very much and will make your visit very special.

● **Drive the Ring of Kerry** (➤ 122) to see some of Ireland's most spectacular coastal and inland scenery, including huge fjord-like bays, the country's highest mountain, sparkling lakes, pretty villages and colourful hedgerows and gardens, which flourish in an exceptionally mild climate.

● **Join in a** *ceilidh,* with traditional music and dancing to get you out of your seat. Lose your inhibitions and get lost in the atmosphere – you can always sing along. There are music sessions in the cities and large towns on most nights. In the country there is usually a session within easy reach, especially in the west and in summer. Wherever you go the standard is generally very high.

● **Wander along Grafton Street** in Dublin, for the shops and the buskers (street musicians), and have a coffee at Bewley's Oriental Café. The variety of open-air acts is enormous, from penny-whistle players to classical string quartets. Check out the small streets off to the side; there are some good pubs to be found.

● **Go to a race meeting at The Curragh**. The Irish have a unique affinity with horses and a day at the races here is quite an experience. Visit the National Stud at Kildare (➤ 94–95) and see the stallions in their stalls and paddocks and learn more at the Irish Horse Museum.

● **Visit Glendalough** to soak up the atmosphere of this historic ruined monastic city (➤ 92–93) in a beautiful valley of the Wicklow Mountains. Only a short drive from Dublin, this is a world apart.

● **Look out from the Cliffs of Moher,** with no other landfall between here and North America, and contemplate the feelings of the millions of emigrants who left this beautiful country for an unknown destiny in the New World (➤ 144).

● **Visit Skibbereen on the day of the cattle market** to sample the real working life of an agricultural community, but do not be in a hurry on the road because you will be following all manner of vehicles

bringing livestock into town – all part of the experience.

● **For a taste of Ireland, eat oysters and drink Guinness** at Paddy Burke's Oyster Inn in Clarenbridge, Co Galway, famous for its oyster festival. To experience the oyster festival, visit Clarenbridge in September.

● **Rent a cruiser and explore the lovely River Shannon,** its lakes and the historic sites, riverside towns and villages along the way (➤ 64). Since the reopening of the Ballyconnell and Ballinamore Canal as the Shannon–Erne Waterway in 1994 it is possible to travel from Belleek in the north through the heart of Ireland to Limerick and the Shannon Estuary.

● **Take a walk along the clifftops of Co Antrim to the Giant's Causeway** to see how ancient travellers would first have witnessed this most remarkable place (➤ 42–43). Drive along this coast for views of cliffs, bluffs, headlands and sandy beaches.

# Planning

Before You Go        22–25

Getting There        26–27

Getting Around       28–29

Being There          30–33

# Before You Go

## WHEN TO GO

| JAN | FEB | MAR | APR | MAY | JUN | JUL | AUG | SEP | OCT | NOV | DEC |
|---|---|---|---|---|---|---|---|---|---|---|---|
| 8°C | 8°C | 10°C | 13°C | 15°C | 18°C | 20°C | 19°C | 17°C | 14°C | 10°C | 8°C |
| 46°F | 46°F | 50°F | 55°F | 59°F | 64°F | 68°F | 66°F | 63°F | 57°F | 50°F | 46°F |

🌧️ 🌧️ 🌧️ ☀️ ☀️ ☀️ 🌧️ ☁️ ☁️ ☁️ 🌧️ 🌧️

⬤ High season   ⬤ Low season

Temperatures are the **average daily maximum** for each month. The best weather is in spring and early summer (April and June). Winter (November to March) can be dark, wet and dreary, especially in the mountainous west, but good-weather days can be magical. In high summer (July and August) the weather is changeable and often cloudy. Autumn (September and October) generally sees good weather. The cities are great places to visit at any time, regardless of the weather, and Christmas and the New Year are particularly popular.

It will almost certainly rain at some time during your stay, no matter when you visit. Be prepared, but try to accept the rain as the Irish do, as a 'wet blessing'.

## WHAT YOU NEED

● Required
○ Suggested
▲ Not required

Some countries require a passport to remain valid for a minimum period (usually at least six months) beyond the date of entry – contact their consulate or embassy or your travel agent for details.

| | UK | Germany | USA | Netherlands | Spain |
|---|---|---|---|---|---|
| Passport (or National Identity Card where applicable) | ▲ | ▲ | ● | ▲ | ● |
| Visa (regulations can change – check before you travel) | ▲ | ▲ | ▲ | ▲ | ▲ |
| Onward or Return Ticket | ○ | ○ | ○ | ○ | ○ |
| Health Inoculations (tetanus and polio) | ▲ | ▲ | ▲ | ▲ | ▲ |
| Health Documentation (► 23, Health Advice) | ● | ● | ● | ● | ● |
| Travel Insurance | ○ | ○ | ○ | ○ | ○ |
| Driving Licence (national) | ● | ● | ● | ● | ● |
| Car Insurance Certificate | ● | ● | ● | ● | ● |
| Car Registration Document | ● | ● | ● | ● | ● |

## ADVANCE PLANNING
### WEBSITES
**Republic of Ireland**
**www**.visitireland.com
**www**.ireland.ie
**www**.corkkerry.ie
**www**.shannon-dev.ie
**www**.irelandwest.travel.ie
**www**.irelandnorthwest.travel.ie
**www**.irelandsoutheast.travel.ie
**www**.midlandseastireland.travel.ie

**Northern Ireland**
**www**.discovernorthernireland.com

## TOURIST OFFICES AT HOME
**In the UK**
Tourism Ireland (for Republic and
Northern Ireland)
103 Wigmore Street,
London W1U 1QF
☎ 0800 0397000
**www**.tourismireland.com

**In the USA** Tourism Ireland
(for Republic and Northern Ireland),
345 Park Avenue, New York,
NY 10154
☎ 212/418-0800

## HEALTH ADVICE
**Insurance**
Nationals of EU and certain other
countries can get discounted
medical treatment in Ireland with a
European Health Insurance Card
(not required for UK nationals),
although private medical insurance
is still advised and is essential for all
other visitors.

**Dental services**
EU nationals or nationals of
countries with which Ireland has a
reciprocal agreement can get
discounted dental treatment within
the Irish health service with a
European Health Insurance Card
(not needed for UK nationals).
Others should take out private
medical insurance.

## TIME DIFFERENCES

|  |  |  |  | |  |
|---|---|---|---|---|---|
| GMT<br>12 noon | Ireland<br>12 noon | → Germany<br>1PM | ← USA (NY)<br>7AM | → Netherlands<br>1PM | → Spain<br>1PM |

Ireland observes Greenwich Mean
Time (GMT), but from late March,
when clocks are put forward one
hour, until late October, summer
time (GMT+1) operates.

PLANNING

## WHAT'S ON WHEN

**February** *Folk Festival:* Gleneagles Hotel, Killarney, Co Kerry.

**March** *Dublin Film Festival.*
*St Patrick's Day:* various parades and pilgrimages commemorating Ireland's patron saint.

**April** *Irish Grand National:* Fairyhouse Racecourse, Co Meath.
*World Irish Dancing Championship:* the best shows, entertainments and parades at various locations.

**April/May** *Beltane Festival:* An Daingean (Dingle).

**May** *Fleadh Nua:* Ennis, Co Clare.
*Belfast Civic Festival and Lord Mayor's Show.*
*Balitmore Seafood and Wooden Boat Festival:* Baltimore, Co Cork.
*Slieve Bloom Walking Festival:* Kinnitty, Co Offaly.
*The Balmoral Show:* Balmoral, Belfast.
*The Cathedral Quarter Arts Festival:* Belfast.

**June** *Limavady Jazz and Blues Festival:* Limavady, Co Londonderry.
*Bloomsday* (16 June): in honour of James Joyce's *Ulysses.*
*Londonderry Walled City Cultural Trail:* Londonderry, Co Londonderry.

**July** *Festival of the Erne:* Belturbet, Co Cavan.
*Galway Arts Festival:* films, music books and plays.
*Boyle Arts Festival:* Boyle, Co Roscommon.
*Historic Sham Fight:* Scarva, Co Down.
*Independence Day Celebrations:* Ulster American Folk Park, Co Tyrone.

**August** *Ballyshannon International Folk Festival:* Ballyshannon, Co Donegal.
*Rose of Tralee Festival:* Tralee, Co Kerry.
*All Ireland Music Festival:* various locations.
*Puck Fair:* Killorglin, Co Kerry.
*Killarney Arts Festival:* Co Kerry.
*Kinsale Regatta and Homecoming Festival:* Co Cork brings expatriates

## NATIONAL HOLIDAYS

| JAN | FEB | MAR | APR | MAY | JUN | JUL | AUG | SEP | OCT | NOV | DEC |
|---|---|---|---|---|---|---|---|---|---|---|---|
| 1 | | 1(3) | (2) | 2 | 1 | 1 | 2 | | 1 | | 2 |

| | |
|---|---|
| **1 Jan** | New Year's Day |
| **17 Mar** | St Patrick's Day |
| **Mar/Apr** | Good Friday, Easter Monday |
| **May** (1st Mon) | May Holiday |
| **May** (last Mon) | Spring Holiday (NI) |
| **Jun** (1st Mon) | June Holiday (RI) |
| **12 Jul** | Orangeman's Day (NI) |
| **Aug** (1st Mon) | August Holiday (RI) |
| **Aug** (last Mon) | Late Summer Holiday (NI) |
| **Oct** (last Mon) | October Holiday (RI) |
| **25 Dec** | Christmas Day |
| **26 Dec** | Boxing Day/St Stephen's Day |

home: sailing, walking and plenty of seafood.

**September** *Clarenbridge Oyster Festival:* Clarenbridge, Co Galway. *Galway International Oyster Festival:* Co Galway. *Blackstairs Blues Festival:* Enniscorthy, Co Wexford. *Story Telling Festival:* Cape Clear, Co Cork. *Listowel Races:* Listowel, Co Kerry. *Appalachian and Blue Grass Festival:* Ulster American Folk Park, Co Tyrone. *Waterford International Festival of Light Opera:* Waterford, Co Waterford. *Proms in the Park:* Donegall Square, Belfast

**October** *Dublin Theatre Festival and Fringe Festival:* the best of Irish and international drama. *Cork Jazz Festival. Cork Film Festival. Kinsale Gourmet Festival:* Co Cork. *Wexford Opera Festival:* Wexford, Co Wexford. *Belfast Festival:* at Queen's.

**November** *Foyle Film Festival:* Londonderry, Co Londonderry. *Listowel Food Fair:* Listowel, Co Kerry.

**December** *Cinemagic Film Festival:* Belfast. *Dingle Wren:* County Kerry. Lots of dressing up and playing tricks on 26 December.

# Getting There

## BY AIR

Scheduled flights operate from Britain, mainland Europe and North America to Dublin, Cork, Knock, Shannon and Belfast. The Republic's national airline is Aer Lingus (☎ 0845 0844 444; www.aerlingus.ie).

**Dublin Airport:** By car, take the M1 south. An Airlink bus leaves from the airport every 20 minutes, more frequently at peak times (moderate fare, under 16s free) to the city centre via the central bus station (Busaras) and Connolly and Heuston railway stations. Taxis wait at the Arrivals area (expensive).

**Belfast International Airport:** The journey to central Belfast takes about 30 to 60 minutes. By car, follow M2 motorway east. An Airbus 300 service (moderate fare, children free) runs every 30 minutes (sometimes hourly on Sundays). Taxi fares are expensive.

**Shannon Airport:** To get to Limerick from Shannon Airport by car, take N18 east. Bus Éireann runs a frequent, inexpensive airport-to-Limerick/Ennis service. Taxis are moderate to expensive.

## BY SEA

Most arrivals by sea come through Dublin Port or Dun Laoghaire south of Dublin; Rosslare, County Wexford, has ferry links with the UK and France.

From Dun Laoghaire port by car to Dublin, simply follow signs for the city centre. There is a frequent Dublin Bus service to Dublin city centre. Taxi fares range from moderate to expensive. An inexpensive DART service (► 28) from Dun Laoghaire to Dublin runs every half-hour (sometimes more frequently).

Belfast Ferryport: the journey to Belfast takes 10 to 15 minutes, depending on traffic. Taxi fares to Belfast city centre are moderate.

Larne Ferryport:

the journey to central Belfast takes 30 to 60 minutes.

## DRIVING

Drive on the left.

Speed limits on motorways (blue): **120kph/75mph**

Speed limits on national roads (green): **100kph/62mph**

Speed limits on regional and local roads (white): **80kph/50mph**

Speed limits on urban roads: **50kph/31mph** (or as signposted)

Seat belts must be worn in front seats at all times and in rear seats where fitted.

Random breath-testing takes place.

Never drink and drive.

Lead replacement petrol (LRP) and unleaded petrol are widely available on both sides of the border. Fuel stations in villages in the Republic stay open until 8 or 9pm, and open after Mass on Sundays. In Northern Ireland, 24-hour petrol stations are fairly common. Fuel is cheaper in Northern Ireland than in the Republic.

If you break down driving your own car and are a member of an AIT-affiliated motoring club, you can call the Automobile Association's rescue service (☎ 1800 667788 in the Republic; ☎ 0800 887766 in Northern Ireland). If the car is rented follow the instructions given in the documentation; most of the international rental firms provide a rescue service.

# Getting Around

## PUBLIC TRANSPORT

### INTERNAL FLIGHTS
Flights from Dublin to other airports in Ireland are operated by Aer Lingus (☎ 0870 876 5000) and Ryanair (☎ 0871 246 0000). Aer Arann (☎ 01-8447700) operates the Aran Flyer with several daily flights between Oiléin Arran (the Aran Islands) and Galway.

### TRAINS
In the Republic a limited network run by Iarnród Éireann (☎ 01-836 6222) serves major towns and cities. Trains are comfortable, generally reliable and fares reasonable. Northern Ireland Railways (☎ 028 9066 6630) operates services from Belfast to main towns and to Dublin.

A light rail overground system, the Dublin Area Rapid Transit (DART), has 30 stations from Howth and Malahide in the north to Greystones in the south (**www.**irishrail.ie). Trains run every 5 minutes in rush hour, otherwise every 10 to 15 minutes. Tickets are available singly from any DART station, but it is more economical to buy them *en bloc* from Dublin Bus (59 Upper O'Connell Street), from some newsstands around the city or at the stations. Tickets need to be validated by stamping them at the machine before going on the platform and boarding a train.

### LONG DISTANCE BUSES
In the Republic, Bus Éireann (☎ 01-836 6111) operates a network of express bus routes serving most of the country (some run summer only). In Northern Ireland, Ulsterbus (☎ 028 9066 6630) has links between Belfast and most villages and towns. Unlimited travel tickets are available.

### URBAN BUSES
City bus services, particularly in Dublin and Belfast, are excellent. Dublin is served by Dublin Bus (☎ 01-8734222) and the Luas, a tram system mainly serving the Dublin surburbs (**www.**luas.ie);

tickets are for Luas or bus. Citybus (☎ 028 9066 6630) serves the Belfast area.

## FERRIES

**Ferries** Two car ferries operate between Ballyhack, Co Wexford and Passage East, Co Waterford (☎ 051-382480) and Killimer, Co Clare and Tarbert, Co Kerry (☎ 065-905 3124), the latter saving 100km (62 miles) on the road journey. There are also ferry services from the mainland to some islands.

## TAXIS

Taxis are available in major towns and cities, at taxi stands or outside hotels, and at main rail stations, ports and airports. In Belfast, black cabs may be shared by customers and some operate rather like buses, shuttling their passengers between the city and the suburbs.
    You cannot hail or stop a taxi in Dublin in the street; instead you have to call them by telephone (look in the *Golden Pages*). The taxis are mostly metered; agree all fares in advance with the drivers of those that are not.

## CAR RENTAL

All of the international car rental firms are represented. A car from a local company, however, is likely to offer cheaper rates, but may not allow different pick-up/drop-off points. Car rental is also less expensive in Northern Ireland than in the Republic.

## CONCESSIONS

**Students** Holders of an International Student Identity Card can buy a Travelsave Stamp which entitles them to travel discounts including a 50 per cent reduction on Bus Éireann, Iarnród Éireann and Irish Ferries (between Britain and Ireland). Contact your local student travel agency for further details. The Travelsave Stamp can be purchased from USIT, 19–21 Aston Quay, O'Connell Bridge, Dublin 2 (☎ 01-6021904).

**Senior citizens** Many car rental companies give discounts to those over 50 or 55, as do some hotels and a few tourist attractions. Some tour companies offer special spring and autumn package deals.

# Being There

## TOURIST OFFICES

### REPUBLIC OF IRELAND
● Dublin Tourism, Suffolk Street, Dublin 2 ☎ 01-6057700; www.dublin.com
● Southeast Tourism, 41 The Quay, Waterford ☎ 051-875788; www.southeastireland.com
● Cork-Kerry Tourism, Grand Parade, Cork City ☎ 021-4255100; www.corkkerry.ie
● Shannon Development, Tourism Division, Shannon Town Centre, Co Clare ☎ 061-361555; www.shannon-dev.ie
● Ireland West Tourism, Forster Street, Galway City ☎ 091-537700; www.irelandwest.ie
● Northwest Tourism, Temple Street, Sligo ☎ 071-916 1201; www.irelandnorthwest.ie
● East Coast & Midlands Tourism, Clonard House, Dublin Road, Mullingar, Co Westmeath ☎ 044-48650; www.eastcoastmidlands ireland.com

### NORTHERN IRELAND
● Tourist Information Centre, St Anne's Court, 59 North Street, Belfast BT1 1NB
☎ 028 9023 1221;
www.discovernorthernireland.com

## EMBASSIES AND CONSULATES
**UK** ☎ 01-205 3700
**Germany** ☎ 020 7824 1300 (NI), 01-269 3011 (RI)
**USA** ☎ 028 9032 8239 (NI), 01-668 8777 (RI)
**Netherlands** ☎ 028 9077 9088 (NI), 01-269 3444 (RI)
**Spain** ☎ 028 9070 9348 (NI), 01-283 9900 (RI)

## TELEPHONES
Public telephone boxes, blue and grey in the Republic and red in Northern Ireland, are being replaced by glass and metal booths.
To make a call, lift the handset, insert the correct coins (RI: 10, 20 or 50 cents, or €1; NI: 10, 20 or 50 pence, or £1) or phonecard and dial.

## EMERGENCY TELEPHONE NUMBERS
**Police** 999
**Fire** 999
**Ambulance** 999
**Coastal rescue** 999

## OPENING HOURS

● Shops    ● Banks      ● Museums
● Offices    ● Post Offices    ● Pharmacies

| 9 AM | 10 AM | 11 AM | 12 PM | 1 PM | 2 PM | 3 PM | 4 PM | 5 PM | 6 PM |

In addition to the times shown above, some shops stay open till 8 or 9pm for late-night shopping on Thursday and Friday. Smaller towns and rural areas have an early closing day on one day a week. Nearly all banks are closed on Saturday and many post offices close at 1pm.

The opening times of museums and tourist sites vary and are subject to change; always check with a local tourist office. Many places close from October to March or have very limited opening, although most major sights are open all year.

### INTERNATIONAL DIALLING CODES

From Ireland to:
**UK:** 00 44 (RI only; no code needed from NI)
**Germany:** 00 49
**USA:** 00 1
**Netherlands:** 00 31
**Spain:** 00 34

### POSTAL SERVICES

**Post offices** The main post offices in O'Connell Street, Dublin, and Castle Place, Belfast, are open extended hours, otherwise

hours are:
Open: 9am
Closed: 5:30pm
(Sat: 1pm/RI, 12.30pm/NI)
☎ 01-705 7000 (RI)
☎ 028 9032 3740 (NI)

### ELECTRICITY

The power supply is:
230 volts (RI);
240 volts (NI).

**Type of socket:** three square-pin (UK type). Parts of the Republic also have 2 round-pin (continental type). Overseas visitors are advised to bring a good travel adaptor with them.

## CURRENCY

The monetary units are (in the Republic), the euro, and (in Northern Ireland) the pound sterling (£). These are not interchangeable. Euro notes come in denominations of 500, 200, 100, 50, 20, 10 and 5; coins in denominations of 2 and 1 euros, 50, 20, 10, 5, 2 and 1 cents. Pound sterling notes for Northern Ireland are issued by the Bank of England in denominations of 50, 20, 10 and 5; coins are available in denominations of £2 and £1, 50, 20, 10, 5, 2 and 1 pence. Provincial banks also issue notes in denominations of 50, 20, 10 and 5, but these are not accepted in other parts of the UK.

## TAX-FREE SHOPPING

Non-EU visitors to Ireland (both the Republic and Northern Ireland) can shop tax-free in stores where you see the Tax-Free sticker. Ask for a cashback voucher every time you make a purchase. Present these vouchers at the cashback desk at Dublin or Shannon airports for an immediate refund. For other departure points ask the store for a pre-paid cashback envelope and then send your vouchers for a cheque or credit card refund.

## HEALTH AND SAFETY

**Sun advice** May and June are the sunniest months, though July and August are the hottest. During these months you should take the normal precautions against the sun.

**Drugs** Prescription and non-prescription drugs are available from pharmacies. In an emergency, contact the nearest hospital.

## TIPS/GRATUITIES

| Yes ✓ No ✗ | | |
|---|---|---|
| Restaurants (if service not included) | ✓ | 10% |
| Cafés (if service not included) | ✓ | 10% |
| Hotels (if service not included) | ✓ | 10% |
| Hairdressers | ✓ | £1/€2 |
| Taxis | ✓ | 10% |
| Tour guides | ✓ | £1/€2 |
| Porters | ✓ | 50p/€1 |
| Cloakroom attendants | ✓ | 50p/€1 |
| Toilets | ✗ | |

## CLOTHING SIZES

| Ireland | UK | Rest of Europe | USA | |
|---------|------|------|------|------|
| 36 | 36 | 46 | 36 | |
| 38 | 38 | 48 | 38 | |
| 40 | 40 | 50 | 40 | |
| 42 | 42 | 52 | 42 | |
| 44 | 44 | 54 | 44 | Suits |
| 46 | 46 | 56 | 46 | |
| 7 | 7 | 41 | 8 | |
| 7.5 | 7.5 | 42 | 8.5 | |
| 8.5 | 8.5 | 43 | 9.5 | |
| 9.5 | 9.5 | 44 | 10.5 | |
| 10.5 | 10.5 | 45 | 11.5 | Shoes |
| 11 | 11 | 46 | 12 | |
| 14.5 | 14.5 | 37 | 14.5 | |
| 15 | 15 | 38 | 15 | |
| 15.5 | 15.5 | 39/40 | 15.5 | |
| 16 | 16 | 41 | 16 | |
| 16.5 | 16.5 | 42 | 16.5 | Shirts |
| 17 | 17 | 43 | 17 | |
| 8 | 8 | 34 | 6 | |
| 10 | 10 | 36 | 8 | |
| 12 | 12 | 38 | 10 | |
| 14 | 14 | 40 | 12 | |
| 16 | 16 | 42 | 14 | Dresses |
| 18 | 18 | 44 | 16 | |
| 4.5 | 4.5 | 38 | 6 | |
| 5 | 5 | 38 | 6.5 | |
| 5.5 | 5.5 | 39 | 7 | |
| 6 | 6 | 39 | 7.5 | |
| 6.5 | 6.5 | 40 | 8 | Shoes |
| 7 | 7 | 41 | 8.5 | |

**Safe water** Tap water in Ireland is safe to drink. Bottled water is widely available.

**Personal safety** The national police forces are:
RI – Garda Síochána (pronounced sheekawnah) in black-and-blue uniforms
NI – Police Service of Northern Ireland in dark green uniforms.
● Be wary in suburban areas of Belfast, southern Co Armagh and Coalisland, Co Tyrone, which are prone to sectarian violence.
● Take care of personal property in Dublin and avoid leaving property visible in cars.

## PHOTOGRAPHY
**Best times to photograph:** early morning and late evening. Irish light can be dull so you may need faster film eg 200 or 400 ASA.
**Restrictions:** in Northern Ireland photographing military installations, vehicles or personnel and inside museums is prohibited.

# Best places to see

Brú na Boinne 36–37

Clonmacnoise 38–39

Corca Dhuibhne
(The Dingle Peninsula) 40–41

The Giant's Causeway 42–43

Kilkenny 44–45

Muckross House 46–47

The National Museum, Dublin 48–49

Oileáin Árann (The Aran Islands) 50–51

The Rock of Cashel 52–53

Ulster-American Folk Park 54–55

# 1 Brú na Boinne

**The valley of the River Boyne east of Slane is a remarkable area containing evidence of Ireland's most ancient history.**

This great neolithic cemetery consists of at least 40 burial sites, and the landscape is dotted with standing stones and earthworks, but the crowning glory is the great passage grave at **Newgrange**. Older than Stonehenge, it is a mound of enormous dimensions, 11m (36ft) high and 90m (295ft) across, with a white quartzite retaining wall encircled with large kerbstones (curbstones) at its base, incised with geometric patterns. Beyond this are the 12 surviving stones of a great circle that once stretched all the way around the mound.

The entrance to the tomb is marked by a massive stone with triple spiral ornamentations, and above it is an opening through which the rays of the rising sun illuminate the interior of the central chamber for about 15 minutes on just one day of the year – the winter solstice, 21 December (the phenomenon is re-created with artificial light the rest of the year, at the end of the guided tour).

Inside the chamber it is possible to see the intricate construction of the roof, which still keeps out water after about 5,000 years, and the recesses into which the remains of the cremated dead were placed, together with final offerings. There are more of the mysterious geometric patterns on the stones. Much about Newgrange remains a mystery, but there is an interpretive centre at the site which explains what has been discovered.

Try to visit Newgrange outside the peak summer season, when it can get uncomfortably crowded, with lengthy queues for the guided tour, and around the winter solstice, when it is almost impossible to get in. People book years in advance to witness the illumination of the chamber on that morning.

The other major sites of Brú na Boinne are the two burial chambers at **Knowth,** northwest of Slane, and the larger site at Dowth, which now can only be viewed from the road.

### Newgrange and Knowth

➕ 9A ✉ Donore ☎ 041-988 0300 🕐 Mar–Apr, Oct daily 9.30–5.30; May, late Sep daily 9–6.30; Jun to mid-Sep daily 9–7; Nov–Feb daily 9.30–5. Closed 23–27 Dec. Knowth: early April–Oct 💲 Varies according to site; visitor centre expensive 🍴 Coffee shop (€)

# 2 Clonmacnoise

**One of the most atmospheric places in Ireland, this ancient monastic city stands in peaceful seclusion beside the River Shannon.**

In AD545 St Ciaran (or Kieran) founded a monastery in this isolated place, cut off from the rest of Ireland by the wide River Shannon and surrounding bogland, and accessible only by boat. In this remote location his monastery grew into an ecclesiastical city, the most important religious foundation of its time in Ireland, and as his burial site it became a place of pilgrimage.

Over the ensuing centuries more and more buildings were added, and the ruins we see today are the most extensive of their kind in the country, including a cathedral, eight churches which were built between the 10th and 13th centuries, two round towers, three high crosses, over 600 early Christian grave slabs, two holy wells and a 13th-century castle. A short distance away is the beautiful Romanesque 'Nun's Church', which was built by Devorgilla, wife of chieftain Tiernan O'Rourke. It was her abduction by Dermot MacMurrough, King of Leinster, that led to conflict which resulted in the Anglo-Norman invasion of Ireland.

Clonmacnoise was also the burial place of the Kings of Connaught and of Tara, including the last High King of Ireland, Rory O'Conor, who was laid to rest here in 1198.

In spite of the remoteness of its setting, Clonmacnoise was known throughout Europe as a centre of excellence in art and literature. Masterpieces of Irish craftsmanship and intricate decoration produced here include the gold and silver Crozier of Clonmacnoise and the Cross of Cong, now in the Treasury of the National Museum in Dublin (➤ 48–49), and the earliest known manuscript in the vernacular Irish, the *Book of the Dun Cow*, was produced here.

➕ 18M ✉ Shannonbridge ☎ 090-96 74195 💲 Mid-Mar to mid-May, Sep to Oct daily 10–6; mid-May to Sep daily 9–7; Nov to mid-Mar daily 10.30–5.30 ✋ Moderate 🍴 Coffee shop end Mar–Oct (€)

# 3 Corca Dhuibhne (The Dingle Peninsula)

**Of all the glories of the west coast, the Dingle Peninsula is the most beautiful and the most dramatic.**

The Dingle Peninsula has many attractions, but best of all is its wonderful coastal scenery; which can be appreciated from the Dingle Way long-distance footpath (49km/31 miles). Along the north coast are great sweeping bays, backed by huge brooding mountains; the south has pretty little coves and the lovely Inch

beach, and in the west is the incomparable sight of the Blasket Islands off Slea Head. After exploring the coast, the drive across the Connor Pass north from Dingle and over Mount Brandon opens up a whole new perspective, with magnificent views down towards Brandon Bay.

Dingle is the main centre, a delightful town of brightly painted houses and shops with a picturesque harbour which still supports a working fishing fleet as well as pleasure craft. These include boat trips to see the famous friendly dolphin, Fungi, who lives near the harbour mouth. Dingle is a lively place with an annual cultural festival and regatta.

Ancient sites on The Dingle include a cliff-top Iron-Age fort near Ventry, Minard Castle, above Dingle Bay, and Gallarus Oratory, a tiny church dating from around the 8th century, between Ballyferriter and Ballynana. Nearby Kilmalkedar

Church, dating from the 12th century, contains the
Alphabet Stone, inscribed with both Roman and
ancient Irish characters.

➕ 14J 🖼 Dingle Bay Eco Tours, The Pier, Dingle
(☎ 086-2858802) operate sea tours around Dingle
Peninsula, including Blasket Islands (Apr–Oct)
ℹ Dingle Tourist Office: The Quay (☎ 066-9151188)

# 4 The Giant's Causeway

**www.**ntni.org.uk

**This unique geological phenomenon, set on a coastline of outstanding beauty, is one of the wonders of the natural world.**

About 40,000 columns of basalt cluster on the shoreline here, forming stepping stones from the cliffs down to the water. Most of them are hexagonal, but some have four, five, seven or eight sides, and the tallest rise to around 12m (39ft). The only other place in the world where such columns can be seen is on Staffa, an island off the coast of Scotland, and this is because they are part of the same formation. Little wonder that the Causeway has been designated a World Heritage Site.

The columns are the result of volcanic action some 60 million years ago, which caused molten basalt to seep up through the chalky bedrock. When it cooled, the rock crystallized into these regular formations, but it would be easy to believe that the blocks were stacked by some giant hand, driven on in its monumental task by the force of some great purpose.

This, of course, is what the ancient Irish believed and who else could have completed the task but the legendary giant Finn McCool, the Ulster warrior who was said to inhabit this Antrim headland? When he once scooped up a clod of earth to throw at a rival, the place he took it from filled with water to become Lough Neagh, the largest lake in the British Isles, and the clod landed in the Irish sea and became the Isle of Man. According to legend, he built the Causeway so that he could cross the sea to reach the lady giant of his dreams, who lived on Staffa – a tall story in more ways than one.

The reality is equally remarkable, but whatever created the Causeway, it is a magnificent sight, particularly when approached on foot from above. There is a cliff-top path all along this stretch of coastline, which can be joined at Blackrock, 2.5km (1.5 miles) from Causeway Head, or from the **Causeway Visitor Centre.**

The Visitor Centre is on the cliff top and is a good introduction to the site. It includes an audio-visual theatre, where a 25-minute show tells the story of the formation of the Causeway. There is also an exhibition area with displays including birdlife and the legend of Finn McCool. A mini-bus runs from here to the Causeway at regular intervals in the summer and guided tours are available.

Beside the centre is the **Causeway School Museum,** a reconstructed 1920s schoolroom complete with learning aids and toys of the era.

➕ 9F 🚌 172 Ballycastle–Portrush; summer services 177 from Coleraine and 252 from Belfast and Larne 🚊 Portrush (11km/7 miles)

**Causeway Visitor Centre**
✉ 44 Causeway Road, Bushmills ☎ 028 2073 1855
🕐 Daily 10–5 (closes 7 Jul–Aug, 4.30 Nov–Feb) 🖐 Free. Moderate charge for parking and extra charge for audio-visual theatre 🍴 Tea room (€)

**Causeway School Museum**
✉ 52 Causeway Road, Bushmills ☎ 028 2073 1777
🕐 Jul–Aug daily 11–5 🖐 Inexpensive

# 5 Kilkenny

**Narrow medieval streets and alleys linking the great castle and cathedral bear witness to Kilkenny's rich history and architectural heritage.**

Standing on a bend of the River Nore, Kilkenny is one of Ireland's most beautiful towns, with pretty little streets to explore, high quality craft studios and an exceptional range of historic buildings.

In medieval times, the town rivalled Dublin in importance and the great **castle** here was the stronghold of the most powerful family in Ireland at the time, the Butlers, Earls and Dukes of Ormonde. Though its origins are back in Norman times, the castle was adapted over the centuries and now reflects the splendour of the 1830s, enhanced by the Butler Gallery of Contemporary Art in the former servants' quarters, the Medieval Room in the South Tower and a cultural facility.

Opposite the castle is the **Kilkenny Design Centre** (▶ 109), which was established in the 1960s to bring Irish craftsmanship to new heights of excellence. Not only was the centre resoundingly successful, it became the spearhead of a crafts revival that has attracted fine craft workers from all over the world. **Rothe House,** a Tudor mansion on three sides of a cobbled courtyard, is also worth a visit. Here you'll find a range of restored rooms, the city and county museum and a costume collection.

Kilkenny originally grew up around the 6th-century monastery founded by St Canice, to whom the cathedral is dedicated. Built on the site of the original monastery, it remains one of the finest 13th-century buildings in Ireland and contains

impressive monuments of black Kilkenny marble
and the Cityscope Exhibition. Beside the cathedral
is the well-preserved round tower of the original
monastery, which gives great views over the city.

✚ 19K 🚉 Kilkenny 1.5km (1 mile)
ℹ Shee Alms House, Rose Inn Street (☎ 056-7751500)

**Kilkenny Castle**
✉ The Parade ☎ 056-7721450 🕐 Jun–Sep daily 9.30–7;
Apr–May daily 10.30–5; Oct–Apr daily 10.30–12.45, 2–5
(guided tours only) 🖐 Moderate 🍽 Tea room May–Sep (€)

**Kilkenny Design Centre**
✉ Castle Yard ☎ 056-7722118 🕐 Apr–Dec Mon–Sat 9–6,
Sun 10–6; Jan–Mar Mon–Sat 9–6 🍽 Restaurant (€)

**Rothe House**
✉ Parliament Street ☎ 056-7722893 🕐 Mar–Nov
Mon–Sat 10.30–5, Sun 3–5; Dec–Feb Mon–Sat 1–5, Sun
3–5 🖐 Moderate

# 6 Muckross House

**Among Ireland's foremost stately homes, Muckross has folk and farm museums and beautiful gardens – all within the Killarney National Park.**

When Henry Arthur Herbert, Member of Parliament for Co Kerry, built his Elizabethan-style mansion in 1843, he could not have found a more perfect site, looking out towards Muckross Lake and surrounded by wonderful scenery that was destined to become a national park. Maud Bowers Bourne was given the house as a wedding present in 1911. Her family presented the house and estate to the Irish nation in 1932 in her memory.

While the house sums up the lifestyle of the landed gentry in Victorian times, the servants' quarters have been converted into a museum of Kerry folk life, with displays and a weaver's workshop. The new Muckross Craft Centre comprises weaving, pottery and bookbinding workshops. There is also a restaurant and gift shop. Out in the grounds, a 28ha (69-acre) farm has been constructed to show farming methods that were used before mechanisation. The rare Kerry cow, a small, black, hardy animal, is being bred here in order to save the herd from extinction.

The gardens at Muckross are renowned for their beauty. Many tender and exotic species thrive in the mild climate, and there are lovely water and rock gardens. A number of nature trails of various lengths begin here, from a one-hour stroll to a

16km (10-mile) circular Heritage Trail through the most extensive natural yew woods in Europe.

➕ 15H ✉ 5km (3 miles) south of Killarney ☎ 064-31440
🕐 House and Gardens: Nov to mid-Mar 9–5.30; mid-Mar to Oct 9–6 (to 7 pm Jul–Aug). Farm: mid-Mar, Apr, May, Sep daily 1–6; Jun–Aug daily 9–6. Closed winter ✋ House and Farm expensive; House moderate; Gardens free 🍴 Cafe (€)
🚌 From Killarney ❓ Horse-drawn jaunting cars from Killarney to the house

7

# The National Museum, Dublin

**www.**museum.ie

**Three locations in Dublin house the magnificent and varied collections and priceless treasures of the National Museum.**

The oldest of the trio (1857) is the Natural History Museum in Merrion Street, which has one of the finest zoological collections in the world. The ground floor has collections relating to native Irish wildlife, while the upper floor has the World Collection, with many African and Asian species, al overlooked by the skeleton of a 20m (65ft)

whale. Here too is a wonderful collection of glass reproductions of marine specimens.

The Kildare Street branch houses the archaeological collections. The centrepiece is a glittering display of ancient gold dating from about 2200 to 700BC. Some of the gold bears faint traces of Celtic decoration, but the best examples of this are to be found in the National Treasury in the adjacent room. Some of the patterns, worked in silver and gold many centuries ago, are almost too tiny to be appreciated by the naked eye. There is a huge collection of Viking artefacts, many found during the redevelopment of Wood Quay. The Road to Independence is an evocative exhibition featuring the events and consequences of the Easter Rising and the Civil War.

Across the city, on the north bank of the River Liffey, the restored Collins Barracks house the National Museum's collection of decorative arts, and displays relating to social, political and military history. These include costumes and jewellery, weaponry and furniture, silver, ceramics and glassware, and interactive multimedia terminals provide more interpretation. There is also an interesting section explaining how the museum goes about the process of research, restoration and conservation of its treasures.

➕ *Dublin 8b* ✉ Kildare Street, Merrion Street, Benburb Street ☎ 01-6777444 🕐 Tue–Sat 10–5, Sun 2–5 ✋ Free
🍴 Cafés at Kildare Street and Collins Barracks (€)
🚌 Cross-city buses 🚉 Pearse station 5-min walk; Heuston Station for Collins Barracks ❓ Guided tours depart from the main entrance at regular intervals

# 8 Oileáin Árann (Aran Islands)

**Bleak and virtually treeless, these three remote islands on the very edge of Europe have a fascinating cultural heritage.**

From the mainland, the distant sight of the three Aran Islands is mysterious and inviting. The west coast of Ireland may seem a remote outpost of Europe, and yet here is something beyond – a place where Gaelic is still the first language, old traditions live on and a small population still scratches a living from the often inhospitable land. Summer visitors are important to the economy, as is the sale of Aran knitwear.

Of the three islands – Inis Mór (Inishmore), Inis Meáin (Inishmaan) and Inis Oírr (Inisheer) – Inis Mór is the largest, and Cill Rónáin (Kilronan) is its main settlement. **Aran's Heritage Centre,** with exhibitions, crafts and an audiovisual show, will steer you towards the many attractions of the islands, from their wonderful beaches to the plentiful historic sites.

There is evidence of prehistoric settlement on the islands. Inis Mór has no fewer than five stone forts, including the dramatic Dún Aonghasa, perched above a 91m (298ft) drop to the sea, and Dún Eochla on the island's highest point.

More atmospheric still are the early Christian sites. The islands have a number of ancient churches, including Teampall Bheanáin, which was built in the 6th century, and Teampall Chiaráin, dating from the 8th or 9th centuries.

The islands deserve more than just a day trip, which can only scratch the surface of what they have to offer.

➕ 15M 🚌 No public transport on the islands ✈ Aer Arann (☎ 091-593034; www.aerarannislands.ie) operates flights taking 10 minutes from Connemara Airport, Co Galway. May–Aug every 30 mins (last flight 7pm); Sep–Apr less frequent ⛴ Island Ferries (☎ 091-568903) operates several sailings daily from Rossaveal, Co Galway

**Aran's Heritage Centre**

✉ Kilronan, Inis Mór ☎ 099-61355 🕐 Jun–Aug daily 10–7; Apr–May, Sep–Oct daily 11–5 ✋ Inexpensive

# The Rock of Cashel

**Ancient seat of the kings of Munster and medieval religious centre, the Rock of Cashel is an awe-inspiring sight.**

This single craggy hill, rising out of the surrounding plain and topped by a cluster of wonderful medieval buildings, dominates the skyline. It is a great landmark that draws more than the eye – its romantic outline of ruined towers and graceful arches seems to beckon from a distance.

The great rock was the obvious choice as the fortress of the kings of Munster, who ruled the southern part of Ireland, and Cashel came to prominence in the 4th or 5th century AD. Legend has it that St Patrick came here to baptize the king, and that during the ceremony, the saint accidentally drove the sharp end of his crozier through the king's foot. The king bore the pain unflinchingly because he believed it to be part of the initiation.

The dominant building on the rock is the 13th-century St Patrick's Cathedral, roofless now, but still impressive, with its long nave and chancel and a 26m (85ft) tower. Inside is a wealth of monuments, including important tombs, and the west end is formed by a 15th-century castle, built as the Archbishop's residence.

The Round Tower and Cormac's Chapel are the oldest structures on the Rock, dating from the 11th to 12th centuries, and the chapel contains a remarkable stone sarcophagus carved with sophisticated Celtic patterns.

One of the later buildings, the 15th-century Hall of the Vicars, is one of the first you see on the Rock, with a display of stone carvings in its vaulted undercroft and above it a splendid hall with a minstrels' gallery, huge fireplace and wonderful timbered ceiling.

✚ 18K ✉ Rock of Cashel ☎ 062-61437 🕐 Mid-Mar to mid-Jun daily 9.30–5.30; mid-Jun to mid-Sep daily 9–7; mid-Sep to mid-Oct daily 9–5.30; mid-Oct to mid-Mar daily 9–4.30 🚻 Moderate 🚌 Dublin–Cork buses ❓ Guided tours on request. Audiovisual, Jun–Sep

# 10 Ulster-American Folk Park

**www.**folkpark.com

**The lives and experiences of Ulster emigrants to the New World are authentically re-created at this splendid open-air museum.**

In a great tide of emigration during the 18th and 19th centuries, over 2 million people left Ulster for a different life in the New World. Among them was five-year-old Thomas Mellon, who went on to become a judge and founder of the Pittsburgh dynasty of bankers, and it is around his childhood home that this museum has been created. Buildings have been reconstructed on the site, giving a complete picture of the world that the emigrants left behind and the one that was awaiting them on the other side of the Atlantic.

The Ulster section includes a typical one-room cottage of the late 18th century, a forge and weaver's cottage, schoolhouse and post office, places of worship and a 19th-century street of shops, with original Victorian shopfronts. Houses include the boyhood homes of John Joseph Hughes, the first Roman Catholic Archbishop of New York, and Robert Campbell, who became a fur trader in the Rockies and a successful merchant in St Louis.

On the dockside, visitors can see a typical merchant's office and a boarding house, where emigrants would await their sailing, then board a reconstruction of the kind of sailing ship which carried them to their new lives.

Beyond this you emerge into the American section of the park, with log houses and barns, including a replica of the six-roomed farmhouse that Thomas Mellon's father built. The buildings contain over 2,000 19th-century artefacts collected in Pennsylvania and Virginia.

🕀 8D 🖂 2 Mellon Road, Castletown ☎ 028 8224 3292
🕔 Apr–Sep Mon–Sat 10.30–6, Sun and public hols 11–6;
Oct–Mar Mon–Fri 10.30–5. Last admission 90 mins
before closing ♿ Moderate 🍴 Cafe (€) 🚌 273
Belfast–Londonderry ❓ Special events to celebrate the
Ulster-American connection are held throughout the year.
Special celebrations on Independence Day, 4 July

# Best things to do

Good places to have lunch          58–59

Ways to be a local                 60–61

Stunning scenery                   62–63

Top activities                     64–65

Boat trips                         66–67

Best souvenirs                     68–69

Places to take the children        70–71

Traditional music                  72–73

A walk around Dublin               74–75

Following the literary greats      76–77

# Good places to have lunch

### Ahernes (€–€€)
Ahernes has a world reputation for its fine seafood dishes.
✉ 163 North Main Street, Youghal, Co Cork ☎ 024-92424

### Ballymaloe House (€€)
Here, at the home of the Ballymaloe Cookery School, local produce is used to produce excellent, good-value food.
✉ Shanagarry Midleton, Co Cork ☎ 021-4652531

### Eccles Hotel (€–€€)
Charming Victorian hotel, where good food can be enjoyed while overlooking Bantry Bay.
✉ Glengarriff, Co Cork ☎ 027-63003

### The Edge (€€)
Feast on delectable dishes prepared with local produce, while

enjoying panoramic views over the River Lagan.
✉ Mays Meadow, Laganbank Road, Belfast ☎ 028 9032 2000

### Harvey's Point (€€)
Great food in a wonderful location on the edge of Lough Eske.
✉ Lough Eske, Donegal ☎ 074-9722208

### Nick's Warehouse (££)
Superb food in a popular, modern venue. The daily changing menu is dedicated to local and organic producers and there is an excellent wine list.
✉ 35–39 Hill Street, Belfast ☎ 028 9043 9690

### The Oliver St John Gogarty (€€)
Traditional Irish food and a lively atmosphere in a historic pub in Temple Bar. Try mussels cooked in wine and Bailey's sauce.
✉ 58–59 Fleet Street, Temple Bar, Dublin ☎ 01-671 1822

### Paddy Burke's (€–€€)
Paddy Burke's is famous as the focal point of the popular Clarenbridge Oyster Festival, so it is not surprising that its speciality dish is shellfish.
✉ Clarenbridge, Co Galway ☎ 091-796226

### Patrick Guilbaud (€€€)
One of the finest restaurants in the city offering superb classic French cuisine in elegant surroundings, featuring a fine collection of Irish art. Popular with business clients.
✉ 21 Upper Merrion Street, Dublin ☎ 01-676 4192

### Ramore Wine Bar (££)
A popular restaurant right on the harbour, offering excellent food and a good wine list.
✉ The Harbour, Portrush, Co Antrim ☎ 028 7082 4313

# Ways to be a local

**Relax** – the local saying is that God created time, then he gave the Irish more of it.

**Talk** – strike up conversation wherever you go. No Irish person would walk into an occupied room without saying something to someone.

**Do not take things too seriously** – the Irish are renowned for their sense of humour and storytelling.

**Develop a taste for Guinness** – it somehow makes you feel you belong. And be patient – it takes a long time to pour a good pint.

**Be subtle** – the Irish tend not to be loud and brash, so make your enquiries soft and your conversation easy.

**Be genuine** – the Irish are usually really interested in what you have to say.

**Know how to let your hair down** – that laid-back attitude seems to evaporate when the time comes to have a 'hooley'.

**Forget the old Hollywood myths and stereotypes** – there may be a degree of unsophistication in the rural areas, but the Irish are generally outward-looking and forward-thinking.

**Do not mind the weather** – though Ireland has a mild climate, there is a strong possibility that you will be rained on at some point. Head for a cosy bar and wait for the sun to reappear.

**Forget your diet** – the Irish know how to fill a plate, particularly at breakfast time, and it all tastes too good to pass up.

# Stunning scenery

**The Beara Peninsula (➤ 118–119)**

**The Cliffs of Moher (➤ 144)**

**Connemara (➤ 145)**

**Corca Dhuibhne (The Dingle Peninsula) (➤ 40–41)**

**The Giant's Causeway (➤ 42–43)**

Glendalough (► 92–93)

The Glens of Antrim (► 172)

The Mountains of Mourne (► 177)

The Ring of Kerry (► 122)

The Wicklow Mountains (► 102)

# Top activities

**Angling:** Ireland is one of the outstanding angling destinations in Europe. There are opportunities for beginners and experts alike and information of all aspects of angling can be found on the website of **Central Fisheries Board** at **www.cfb.ie**

**Birdwatching:** With over 420 species of birds recorded in Ireland and wonderfully diverse habitats there is plenty for the avid birdwatcher to see. Eric Dempsey, an Irish Tourist Board (Faílte Ireland) approved guide, runs a variety of birding tours throughout the country. Check out his website for all the details at **www.**birdsireland.com

**Cruising on the Shannon or Erne waterways:** Try your hand at inland cruising by taking out a small boat, then pulling up at night at a pub. Most of the length of the River Shannon is navigable and the Shannon-Errne Waterway links the river to Lough Erne.

**Cycling:** Ireland is a great place to get on your bicycle, with quiet rural roads and some spectacular moutain and coastal rides. The west and southwest are particularly good for cycling routes.

**Gaelic sports:** The Irish are passionate about their traditional sports. The most watched sporting event in Ireland is the Gaelic football All-Ireland final held in September in Dublin. The game is very fast, a cross between rugby and football. Hurling is specific to Ireland and is popular everywhere.
**Cumann Luthchleas Gael** ✉ Pairc an Chrocaigh, Dublin 3 ☎ 01-8363222
**Gaelic Athletic Association** ✉ Belfast ☎ 028 3752 1907

**Golf:** There are over 400 golf courses in Ireland. The Republic of Ireland's golfing body can give details on all Ireland's courses.
**Golfing Union of Ireland** ✉ Unit 8, Block G, Maynooth Business Campus, Maynooth, Co Kildare ☎ 01-505 4000; www.gui.ie

**Horse racing:** This is very popular in the Republic of Ireland. There are 27 racecourses and races are held nearly every day. Contact **Horse Racing Ireland** ☎ 045-842800; www.hri.ie

**Horse-back riding:** The affinity between the Irish and horses is legendary, and there are hundreds of places around the country where you can enjoy lovely scenery on horseback. For further information contact: **Association of Irish Riding Establishments** (AIRE) ✉ 11 Moore Park, Newbridge, Co Kildare ☎ 045-431584

**Sailing:** You'd be hard pushed to find a part of Ireland's coastline where there isn't a local sailing club nearby. To locate a club contact the **Irish Sailing Association** (www.sailing.ie).

**Walking:** Every region of Ireland offers great walking opportunities and the local tourist offices have information for area hikes. Some towns celebrate with annual walking festivals such as the one in Kenmare, Co Kerry, in late May.

# Boat trips

One of the best ways to see the diversity of coast, island and river scenery is to go on a boat trip. Contact the following companies directly or check with the local tourist office. Most trips are May to October only.

**Báan Daingin (Dingle Bay) and Fungi the Dolphin** (Booking office: Dingle Bay Ferries, Dunromen, Lispole, Co Kerry)

**Cork Harbour from Cobh** (Booking office: Marine Transport Services, Atlantic Quay, Cobh)

**Killarney Lakes from Ross Castle** (Booking office: Killarney Watercoach Cruises, 3 High Street, Killarney, Co Kerry)

**Lough Corrib and Inchagoill Island** (Booking office: Tourist office, Eyre Square, Galway)

**Lough Derg–Killaloe** (Booking office: Derg Maine, Kilaloe, Co Clare)

**Lough Key Forest Park** (Booking office: Lough Key Boat Tours, Rockingham Harbour, Lough Key Forest Park, Boyle, Co Roscommon)

**Lough Ree–Athlone** (Booking office: Shannon Holidays, Jolly Mariner, Maine, Athlone, Co Westmeath)

**River Erne from Belturbet** (Booking office: Tarbot Tours, Deanery Park, Belturbet, Co Cavan)

**Skelligs from Valencia** (Booking office: The Skellig Experience, Valencia Island, Co Kerry)

**Waterford–Carrick-on-Suir Castle** (Booking office: Gallery Cruising Restaurant, Bridge Quay, New Ross, Co Wexford)

# Best souvenirs

**Aran knitwear** – the distinctive patterns of the traditional Aran sweater are known all over the world. They are still produced in the Oileáin Árann (Aran Islands).

**Belleek pottery** – the famous basket-weave pottery has been made at the west end of Loch Erne in Co Fermanagh since 1857 and the same traditional methods are still employed. Take a tour of the factory and you can see the craftspeople at work and then visit the vistor's centre and shop.

**Claddagh rings** – found in shops throughout Ireland, traditional Celtic designs are popular, in particular the Claddagh ring, a design dating from the 17th century. The ring consists of a heart encircled by pair of hands with a crown above the heart. It symbolizes love and fidelity.

**Connemara marble** – it has been quarried in Connemara for centuries and you can buy a huge range of items, from massive kitchen worktops to delicate rosary beads and jewellery. Check out Connemara Marble Industries in Moycullen.

**Donegal tweed** – Magee & Co in Donegal town have been manufacturing tweed since 1866; Ardara Heritage Centre tells the story of Donegal tweed and Aran knitwear, and there are tours of hand-loom weaving centres.

**Irish linen** – Banbridge, Co Down is the main centre. The Ferguson Linen Centre has factory tours, and Banbridge is the starting point of Linen Tours, a coach journey around nearby sites, including linen mills and factories. There is also an Irish Linen Centre in Lisburn.

**Irish lace** – lace-making today is a big business, with large factories producing fabric in minutes, but it all stems from a cottage industry and some is still handmade today. Take your pick of local lace. The famous names include Limerick, Kenmare, Youghal and Carrickmacross.

**Irish drinks** – choose from Bushmills, Jameson, Powers and Paddy whiskeys; Guinness, Beamish and Murphy's stout, Smithwick's beer; Cork gin; Bailey's liqueur. Take a tour of the Guinness Storehouse (➤ 84–85) or the Old Jameson Distillery (➤ 87) in Dublin, the Old Bushmills Distillery in Co Antrim or the Jameson Heritage Centre in Midleton, Co Cork.

**Peat carvings** – a unique souvenir crafted from 5,000-year-old Irish turf from some of Ireland's oldest boglands. Choose from jewellery in traditional Celtic designs, clocks, paperweights and more. One producer is Island Turf Crafts in Coalisland, Co Tyrone.

**Waterford crystal** – founded in 1783, the business is now a highly commercial operation but it is still made in the same town and by much the same method as when it was first set up. The factory on the outskirts of Waterford has organized tours (➤ 128).

# Places to take the children

## BALLYPOREEN, CO TIPPERARY
### Mitchelstown Caves
The caves are renowned for their depth of 1km (half a mile), and comprise two groups, Desmond's Cave and New Cave.
✉ Off the N8 4km (2.5 miles) north of Ballyporeen ☎ 052-67246
🕐 Mar–Nov daily 10–6; Dec–Feb 11–4.30 💰 Moderate

## BELFAST
### Belfast Zoo
A modern world-class zoo set in attractive parkland and housing over 160 species of rare and endangered animals.
✉ Off Antrim Road ☎ 028 9077 6277 🕐 Apr–Sep daily 10–5; Oct–Mar daily 10–2.30 💰 Moderate 🍴 Refreshments (£)

### W5
An interactive discovery centre located at the Odyssey in central Belfast. Five exhibition areas: Wow, Start, Go, See and Do.
✉ 2 Queen's Quay ☎ 028 9046 7700 🕐 Mon–Sat 10–6, Sun 12–6 💰 Moderate

## DINGLE, CO KERRY
### Dingle Oceanworld
Underwater life galore. Watch out for the sharks!
✉ Dingle Harbour ☎ 066-9152111 🕐 Jul, Aug 9–8.30; May, Jun, Sep 9–6.30; Oct–Apr 10–5 💰 Expensive

## DUBLIN
### Dublin Zoo
This historic zoo in Phoenix Park makes an ideal family day out.
✉ Phoenix Park ☎ 01-4748900 🕐 Mar–Sep Mon–Sat 9.30–6, Sun 10.30–6;Oct–Feb Mon–Sat 9.30–dusk, Sun 10.30–dusk 💰 Expensive 🍴 Restaurant and cafés

### Viking Splash Tour

Take a tour of Dublin in an ex-World War II amphibious vehicle. It takes in all the main city-centre sights – then heads straight into the waters of Grand Canal Basin to finish the tour afloat.

✉ 64–65 Patrick Street ☎ 01-7076000; www.vikingsplashtours.com
🕐 Every half hour 10–12, 1.30–5. Mar–Oct daily; Feb Wed–Sun; Nov Tue–Sun

## FOTA, CO CORK
### Fota Wildlife Park

Established by the Royal Zoological Society of Ireland, Fota Wildlife Park's primary aim is the breeding of endangered species.

✉ 1.5km (1 mile) south of Cork Harbour ☎ 021-4812678 🕐 Daily 10–5
✋ Expensive

## SALTHILL, CO GALWAY
### Leisureland

A modern pool complex with waterslides, treasure cove, tropical beach pool and playground.

☎ 091-521455 🕐 Mon–Fri 8 am–10 pm, Sat 8–5, Sun 8–6 ✋ Moderate

## SHANNONBRIDGE
### Clonmacnoise & West Offaly Railway

Narrow-gauge railway tour of the Blackwater bog (9km/5.5 miles) with on-board commentary.

☎ 090-9674114 🕐 Apr–Oct daily 10–5, trains leave on the hour. Groups only in winter ✋ Moderate 🍴 Coffee shop (€)

## TRALEE, CO KERRY
### Aqua Dome

Tralee's wonderful waterpark has all the rides you would expect. You can also visit the Blennerville Windmill.

✉ On the Dingle road ☎ Aqua Dome: 066-7128899 🕐 Aqua Dome Mon–Fri 10–10, Sat, Sun 11–8; windmill Apr–Oct 10–6 ✋ Expensive

# Traditional music

Some of the best traditional music nights are the impromptu sessions in local pubs throughout Ireland. Check at the tourist offices for what's likely to be on where. Here are just a few suggestions.

**An Daingean (Dingle)** – a wealth of musical talent can be heard in this area of western Ireland. Among many popular venues in the town are An Chonair, An Droichead, McCarthy's Pub and the Marina Inn.

**Belfast** – the John Hewitt Bar in Donegall Street hosts regular traditional music sessions as well as some nights of jazz. Good food and great for conversation with no television, taped music, juke box or gaming machines.

**Cork** – try the Lobby bar in Union Quay and the Old Oak Bar in Oliver Plunkett Street.

**Doolin** – hot spot in Co Clare for some great music with O'Connor's a favourite. Most of the great names have played here and it has become a bit of an institution. But don't be afraid to sing along – it's a jolly place to go. McGann's by the bridge is another option, a quieter, more serious venue.

**Dublin** – for a bit of musical history go to O'Donoghue's in Merrion Row. Here the music is spontaneous and lively. It's a small venue which gets very crowded and it's where the famous Dubliners folk group started their career back in the early 1960s. Oliver St John Gogarty's in the heart of Temple Bar is a popular venue for traditional music every night of the week and sometimes at lunchtime too.

**Galway** – continuing western Ireland's tradition for great sounds, try Tigh Neachtain in Cross Street.

**Howth** – just to the north of Dublin and a short trip on the DART, you'll find traditional music in this popular fishing village at the Abbey Tavern.

**Kenmare** – there's a great tradition of good Irish music in this attractive little town in Co Kerry. For the closest to the real thing try Crowley's in Henry Street for the best in impromptu sessions. You can find more in the smart surroundings of the Landsdowne Arms Hotel.

**Sligo** – another area known for good traditional music in both the town and local villages – check with the tourist office for venues. Furey's in Sligo is owned by the traditional band Dervish and is worth a visit.

**Westport** – in Co Mayo, popular for its traditional music, you will find Matt Molloy's, owned by Molloy, the flute player of the world-famous folk band the Chieftains, who still often plays here.

# a walk

## around Dublin

**This walk starts in Dublin's most famous shopping street, then takes in many of the city's major attractions.**

*Walk south along Grafton Street, cross the road and enter the gardens of St Stephen's Green, leaving by the small gate at the left corner. Cross the road and go forward along Kildare Street.*

The National Museum, on the right, is Ireland's treasurehouse, with some stunning objects and fascinating exhibitions (➤ 48–49).

*At the end of Kildare Street go left into Nassau Street, then right to College Green with Trinity College on the right (➤ 88–89). Follow Westmoreland Street, walk*

*across O'Connell Bridge and turn left alongside the river.
Cross Ha'penny Bridge (footbridge), then go through
Merchant's Arch into Temple Bar.*

This network of cobbled lanes is worth exploring.

*Turn right into Essex Street East. Take the third left into
Eustace Street. At the end turn right along Dame Street.*

Dublin Castle is on the left, its medieval origins buried
beneath 18th-century reconstructions that house the truly
magnificent State Apartments, including the Throne Room
(► 82).

*Keep forward to Christ Church Cathedral.*

Begun in the 12th century, beautiful Christ Church is the
foremost cathedral in Dublin. Next to it is Dvblinia (► 84).

*Go down Fishamble Street to the river. Turn right along
the south bank, and at O'Connell Bridge turn right and
return to Grafton Street.*

**Distance** About 4km (2.5 miles)
**Time** 3–4 hours
**Start/end point** Grafton Street ✚ *Dublin 7b*
**Lunch** The Auld Dubliner (€) ✉ 24–25 Temple Bar ☎ 01- 6770527

# Following the literary greats

**Samuel Beckett (1906–1989)** – the author and playwright, born and educated in Dublin, was one-time associate and assistant to James Joyce. His play *Waiting for Godot* is probably his most well-known work.

**Seamus Heaney (born 1939)** – this famous poet, born in Mossbawn, Co Londonderry and a graduate of Queen's University, Belfast, went on to be a professor at both Harvard and Oxford universities.

**James Joyce (1882–1941)** – probably the most famous of them all. You can follow his trail throughout Dublin City and there's a day dedicated to his most well-known hero Leopold Bloom, immortalized in *Ulysses*. You will find his statue in Earl Street.

**Patrick Kavanagh (1904–1967)** – the poet was born near Inniskeen, Co Monaghan. Sit next to him on a bench by the Grand Canal in Dublin where he meditates in bronze.

**Edna O'Brien (born 1936)** – gained her insight into the repressive position of women in Irish society from her early days in the rural Catholic village of Tuamgraney in County Clare.

**George Bernard Shaw (1856–1950)** – 'author of many plays' is the simple accolade on the plaque outside Shaw's Birthplace in Syynge Street, close to the Grand Canal in Dublin.

**Bram Stoker (1847–1912)** – the author of the classic Gothic horror tale, *Dracula*, lived and worked in Dublin,

running the Lyceum Theatre in conjunction with the actor
Henry Iriving.

**Jonathan Swift (1667–1745)** – a Dublin man born and bred and
later to become dean of St Patrick's Cathedral, Swift is probably
best known for his satirical work *Gulliver's Travels*.

**Oscar Wilde (1854–1900)** – born in Dublin. You can visit his
house, and be sure not to miss his wonderful reclining statue
in nearby Merrion Square.

**W B Yeats (1865–1939)** – although born in Dublin, Yeats has
connections with other parts of Ireland. He lived for a time at
Thor Ballylee Tower south of Galway and there is an impressive
statue of him (➤ opposite) in the town of Sligo, which hosts an
annual Yeats summer school.

# Exploring

| | |
|---|---|
| **The East** | 81–110 |
| **The South** | 111–136 |
| **The West** | 137–158 |
| **The North** | 159–187 |

It's the diverse nature of Ireland that lives in the memory. From vibrant, cosmopolitan cities to quiet rural backwaters; from coast to mountains, from picture postcard villages to market towns; the country and its people are unique. If you have only time to visit Dublin at least try and take a trip on the DART as in a few minutes you will be along the coast, adding a further dimension to your visit. As in so many countries the cities are only part of the whole and not a true reflection of the country. You won't go anywhere very fast, although the roads are improving annually, but that is part of the charm. People don't rush in Ireland and even in Dublin and Belfast, now cities competing with any other major European destination for culture, restaurants and vibrant nightlife, the locals still have time to stop and chat.

# The East

**The eastern part of Ireland is inevitably dominated by Dublin, a lively city with a lot to see and do, but the east has much more to offer than just the capital. Ireland's most extensive mountain region is just to the south of Dublin in Co Wicklow, where remote, silent valleys and wild exposed mountain tops can be reached in less than half an hour's drive.**

Long sandy beaches and golf links stretch along the coast, which remains unspoilt in spite of the presence of the main ferry ports. The resorts retain an old-fashioned appeal.

Inland, the east has some fascinating places to see. To the north of Dublin is a cluster of historic sites including Tara, Kells and Newgrange.

Southwest of the capital is the horse-racing centre of Kildare and The Curragh and the wonderful old city of Kilkenny, and in the far south are the pretty villages and fine beaches of the Wexford coast.

# Dublin

Part of Dublin's charm is that it only takes a few days of wandering around its attractive streets and leafy squares – and into its atmospheric pubs – to feel that you know the city intimately. And yet, every visit reveals some new delight.

Dublin has everything a capital city should have – magnificent architecture, excellent shopping, lively entertainment and cultural events, superb museums and galleries, colourful parks and gardens and a strong sense of history.

Until now, most of Dublin's attractions have been in the smart areas south of the river. The northside was once a run down area with seedy back streets, but now a redevelopment plan has given it the designer treatment. Wide O'Connell Street has become an attractive, leafy boulevard; behind it in Henry Street the shopping centres have been upgraded and the area now rivals Grafton Street. Smithfield Village is taking shape as an interesting cultural quarter, while the already rejuvenated Temple Bar has continued to grow around Cow's Lane. The docks are being developed and the new LUAS light rail system brings Dubliners in from the suburbs.

✚ 21M

🛈 Suffolk Street (☎ 01-6057700)

## DUBLIN CASTLE

Soon after the Anglo-Normans arrived in Ireland in the 12th century, King John ordered the building of Dublin Castle and it remained the centre of English power in Ireland until 1922. In spite of its great medieval walls and round bastions, much of the castle is a product of the 18th century, including the splendid State Apartments, where presidents are inaugurated and visiting dignitaries received. The Chester Beatty Library, one of the world's best collections of Oriental and European manuscripts, is located in the castle gardens.

✚ *Dublin 5b* ✉ Dame Street ☎ 01-6777129 🕓 Mon–Fri 10–4.45, Sat–Sun and public hols 2–4.45 (state apartments may be closed for functions) 🖐 Moderate 🍴 Self-service restaurant (€) 🚌 Cross-city buses

## DUBLIN WRITERS MUSEUM

No other city in the world has spawned so many writers of international repute, including four Nobel prize winners, and this museum is a celebration of that literary heritage. The displays, in the magnificent surroundings of a restored 18th-century mansion, encompass the whole spectrum of Irish works, from the 8th-century *Book of Kells* to the present, taking in Swift, Sheridan, Shaw, Wilde, Yeats, Joyce and Beckett along the way. One room is devoted entirely to children's literature, and there are regular exhibitions and readings.

✚ *Dublin 6f* ✉ 18/19 Parnell Square North ☎ 01-8722077 🕓 Mon–Sat 10–5 (until 6 Mon–Fri Jun–Aug), Sun and public hols 11–5 ✋ Moderate 🍴 Restaurant (€€) and coffee shop (€) 🚌 10, 11, 11a, 11b, 13, 16a, 19a, 22, 22A, 36 🚊 DART Connolly

## DVBLINIA

Developed by the Medieval Trust, Dvblinia tells the story of the city from the arrival of the Anglo-Normans in the 12th century until the closure of the monasteries in 1540. It is housed in a beautifully preserved old building, the former Synod Hall, linked to Christ Church Cathedral by an ancient covered bridge. There is a model of medieval Dublin and artefacts from the National Museum.

**www.**dublinia.ie

✚ *Dublin 4b* ✉ St Michael's Hill ☎ 01-6794611 ⑧ Apr–Sep daily 10–5; Oct–Mar Mon–Sat 11–4, Sun and public hols 10–3 ♨ Moderate ﹗ Tea rooms Jun–Aug (€) 🚌 51b, 78a, 90, 123

## GUINNESS STOREHOUSE

Guinness, one of the most potent symbols of Irishness, is now brewed all over the world – at a rate of over 10 million glasses a day – and this is where it all started, founded by Arthur Guinness in 1759. As you enter the Storehouse through a stone arch an escalator whisks you to the heart of the building into what is described as a large glass pint. Within this glass structure you journey through the production process. Entertaining displays and audiovisuals give an insight into the history, manufacture and advertising of Dublin's most famous product. You will end your visit in the rooftop bar to sample a free glass of the 'black stuff'.

**www.**guinnessstorehouse.com

🚩 *Dublin 1b* ✉ St James's Gate ☎ 01-4044800 🕐 Daily 9.30–5, (until 8 Jul–Aug) 💷 Expensive 🍴 Brewery bar, Gravity bar 🚌 51b, 78a from Aston Quay; 123 from O'Connell Street

## KILMAINHAM GAOL

In its time both a caution and an inspiration, Kilmainham Gaol stands as a monument to the struggle for Irish independence and those leaders of the 1916 Easter Rising who were imprisoned or executed here. It gives visitors a chillingly realistic impression of what life must have been like for the prisoners who were incarcerated here, be they patriots or petty criminals, from its inauguration in 1796 to 1924.

🚩 *Dublin 1c (off map)* ✉ Inchicore Road, Kilmainham ☎ 01-4535984 🕐 Apr–Sep daily 9.30–5; Oct–Mar Mon–Sat 9.30–4, Sun 10–5. Last tour one hour before closing 💷 Moderate 🚌 51B, 78A, 79 from Aston Quay. Luas: Museum Stop 🚉 Heuston Station

## NATIONAL GALLERY OF IRELAND

First opened in 1864, this wonderful gallery has one of the finest collections of European art in the world. Located in the heart of Georgian Dublin, the gallery contains nearly 2,500 paintings, over 5,000 drawings, watercolours and miniatures, over 3,000 prints and more than 300 pieces of sculpture and *objets d'art*. The Millennium Wing houses a centre for the study of Irish art and an archive dedicated to the paintings of Jack B Yeats (1872–1957).

✚ *Dublin 8b* ✉ Merrion Square West and Clare Street ☎ 01-6615133
🕐 Mon–Sat 9.30–5.30, Thu 9–8.30, Sun 2–5.30. Closed Good Fri, 24–26 Dec
✋ Voluntary 🍴 Restaurant and café 🚌 Cross-city buses 🚊 DART Pearse

## NATIONAL MUSEUM
See pages 48–49.

## NATIONAL WAX MUSEUM
This museum brings to life everyone from Irish historical figures to the cult cartoon family the Simpsons. Here you will find life-size re-creations of heroes such as Robert Emmet, Wolfe Tone, Parnell, the leaders of the 1916 rebellion and former presidents. Literary giants are represented with figures of Joyce, Yeats and their contemporaries. You'll find the obligatory Hall of the Megastars featuring the likes of Madonna and Michael Jackson, and the Chamber of Horrors with accompanying blood-curdling screams, as well as a World of Fairytale and Fantasy. You can see the Popemobile used by Pope John Paul II on his visit to Ireland in 1979 and also the figures of the last four popes.

🚩 *Dublin 5f* ✉ Smithfield Square, Smithfield ☎ 01-8726340 🕐 Call for opening times 💷 Expensive 🚌 67, 68, 69, 79, 90

## OLD JAMESON DISTILLERY
Explore the history of Irish whiskey-making, which goes back to the 6th century, through exhibits and audiovisual presentations on

the site of the old Jameson Distillery in Smithfield Village on the north side of the River Liffey. You can view old and new equipment and watch a working bottling line, then sample a drop of the *uisce beatha*, literally 'water of life'. There is an excellent shop selling a variety of whiskies as well as clothing and posters.

🚩 *Dublin 3d* ✉ Bow Street, Smithfield Village ☎ 01-8173838 🕐 Daily 10–5.30, guided tours only, every 40 mins 💷 Expensive 🍴 Restaurant and bar (€–€€) 🚌 67, 67a , 68, 69, 79, 90. Luas to Smithfield

## TEMPLE BAR

Sooner or later, every visitor to Dublin heads to the area known as Temple Bar, a lively warren of narrow, cobbled streets just south of the Liffey. The word 'bar' means riverside path. There is access from all sides, but the best way in is to walk across the Ha'penny Bridge from the north side of the river and keep straight on through the arch.

You'll find every kind of watering hole and eating place here, from historic pubs like the Oliver St John Gogarty (➤ 59; go for the Sunday brunch music session) to bistros and internet cafés. There are interesting galleries, lively pubs, buskers and music just about everywhere.

✚ *Dublin 6c*

## TRINITY COLLEGE

Through the Palladian façade of Trinity College is not only an oasis of peace and quiet in the heart of the busy city centre, but also one of its finest ranges of buildings.

The college was founded in 1592 by Elizabeth I, with many fine buildings from the 18th and 19th centuries. The finest of them all is the great **Library** (1732), which contains some of Ireland's greatest treasures. Magnificent illuminated manuscripts on display include the 9th-century *Book of Kells* and the *Book of Armagh*.

The main entrance is on College Green, opposite the Bank of Ireland, next to one of the busiest roads in Dublin. On Parliament Square, inside the college grounds, you will find the 19th-century campanile and the elegant 18th-century Dining Hall and the Chapel.

✚ *Dublin 7c*

**Library**

✉ College Green ☎ College: 01-6082320. Library: 01-6081661 ⏰ Mon–Sat 9.30–5, Sun 12.30–4.30 (from 9.30 Jun–Sep). Closed 10 days at Christmas 💰 Campus free; Library and *Book of Kells* expensive 🚌 Cross-city buses

# What to See in the East

**BRÚ NA BOINNE**
See pages 36–37.

**CASTLETOWN HOUSE**
Castletown at Celbridge is Ireland's largest and finest Palladian
country house, built in the 18th century for William Conolly,
Speaker of the Irish House of Commons. The central block,
modelled on an Italian *palazzo*, is linked to its two wings with
gracefully curving colonnades.

The sumptuous interiors, including the Pompeian Gallery, are largely the inspiration of Lady Louisa Lennox, who came to the house on her marriage in 1758. At its heart is a magnificent hall, with sweeping cantilevered staircase and superb plasterwork. Managed by Dúchas, the Irish national Heritage Service.

✚ 21M ✉ Celbridge ☎ 01-6288252 ⏰ Mid-Apr to Sep Mon–Fri 10–6, Sat–Sun and public hols 1–6; Oct Mon–Fri 10–5, Sun and public hols 1–5 ✋ Moderate 🚌 67, 67a from Wellington Quay, Dublin

### CEANANNUS MOR (KELLS)

In AD804 a Columban monastery was founded at Kells by monks who had fled the Viking raids on Iona. It was to become one of the great centres of Celtic Christianity, and it was here that the magnificently decorated version of the Gospels, the *Book of Kells*, was completed. This is now a prized possession of Dublin's Trinity College Library (▶ 88–89) after being moved there during the Cromwellian wars. Replicas are on display in Kells' Heritage Centre, with a multimedia exhibition that entices you to explore the sites throughout Kells.

The town's street pattern reflects the circular shape of the monastery, from which only a round tower and the tiny St Columcille's House remain. The original doorway of the house was 2.4m (8ft) above ground level, a defensive measure which reflected troubled times. Close to the round tower, in the churchyard, are three carved stone crosses, also from the 9th century. A fourth, with 30 decorative panels, stands in Market Square.

✚ 9A ✉ Kells Heritage Centre, The Courthouse, Headfort Place ☎ 046-9247840 ⏰ May–Sep Mon–Sat 10–5.30, Sun and public hols 2–6; Oct–Apr Tue–Sat 10–5 ✋ Moderate

## GLENDALOUGH

Deep in the heart of the Wicklow Mountains (➤ 102) are the atmospheric remains of a remarkable monastic city which was founded in the 6th century by St Kevin and remained an important place of pilgrimage well into the 18th century.

Many legends surround the mysterious St Kevin. He is said to have come to Glendalough to avoid worldly pleasures and the advances of a beautiful redheaded woman with 'unholy eyes', and that he rolled himself, and his putative lover, in stinging nettles to dampen their desire. He may also have hurled the lady into an icy lake to cool her ardour.

Some of the remains, accessible only by boat, are on the south side of the Upper Lake and include the reconstructed Templenaskellig and St Kevin's Bed, a small cave reached after a difficult climb.

The settlement developed mainly between the 10th and 12th centuries, when most of the buildings were erected. These include St Kevin's Church, an oratory known as St Kevin's Kitchen, the 30m (98ft) round tower and the Cathedral of St Peter and St Paul. There are several other churches and buildings around the site, as well as numerous gravestones and crosses, including the plain granite St Kevin's Cross (3.5m/11ft high). The **Visitor Centre** by the first parking area displays many antiquities found in the valley and is the starting point of guided tours.

✚ 21L

**Glendalough Visitor Centre**

☎ 040-445325/445352 🕔 Mid-Mar to mid-Oct daily 9.30–6; mid-Oct to mid-Mar daily 9.30–5 💵 Inexpensive 🚌 Can be reached on coach tours from Dublin (Bus Éireann)

## IRISH NATIONAL HERITAGE PARK

On the River Slaney, a little way west of Wexford, is the Irish National Heritage Park, which re-creates Irish life over a period of about 9,000 years, ending with the Anglo-Norman period. No fewer than 14 historical sites have been re-created amidst the maturing woodland of the 14ha (34.5-acre) site. The trappings and paraphernalia of everyday life through the ages help to  bring it all to life, and the park successfully combines the requirements of tourism with serious historical content.

✚ 21J ✉ Ferrycarrig ☎ 053-20733 🕔 Mar–Oct daily 9.30–6.30; Nov–Feb daily 9.30–5.30 (last admission 3pm) 💵 Moderate 🍴 Restaurant (€€)

## JERPOINT ABBEY

Jerpoint Abbey is one of Ireland's finest monastic ruins. The first religious house here was a Benedictine abbey, founded around 1158, but by 1180 it had been taken over by the Cistercians. Substantial remains of buildings from the 12th to the 15th centuries tower impressively above the main road. For all its size and presence, however, what is most interesting here are the amusing carvings along the restored cloister arcade, the fine monuments and various effigies.

🚌 20K ✉ Thomastown
☎ 056-7724623 🕐 Jun to mid-Sep daily 9.30–6; mid-Sep to end Oct daily 10–5; mid-Mar to mid-May daily 10–4
✋ Inexpensive

## KILDARE

This fine old county town has an attractive central square and some medieval buildings. St Brigid's Cathedral is on the site of a monastery founded in AD490 and nearby is a 10th-century round tower with wonderful views. The other tower in the town is that of the 15th-century castle.

Kildare is at the heart of horse-racing country, and Irish-bred horses are among the most prized in the world. The **National Stud** at Tully House gives visitors an insight into the development and control of these magnificent animals.

The **Japanese Gardens** at Tully House, landscaped in 1906 to 1910 by the Japanese gardener Tasa Eida, include a tea house and a miniature village carved from rock from Mount Fuji. The gardens

symbolize the life of man, taking the pilgrim-soul on a journey from Birth to Eternity.

**St Fiachra's Garden** seeks to re-create the landscape of rocks and water that inspired spirituality in early monastic life. At its heart is a superb bronze statue of St Fiachra, noted for his love of nature, sitting contemplatively, holding up a seed. A stone hermitage contains pieces of sparkling Waterford Crystal representing rocks and flowers.

✚ 20M

**National Stud/Japanese Gardens/St Fiachra's Gardens**

✉ Tully, Kildare ☎ 045-521617 🕓 Mid-Feb to mid-Nov daily 9.30–6
🖐 Expensive 🍴 Restaurant (€€) 🚌 Dublin–Kildare (bus stops at gate)

## KILKENNY
See pages 44–45.

## MALAHIDE
The town of Malahide is a traditional seaside resort that has also become a popular residential area for commuters to Dublin. One of its great attractions is that it is particularly well endowed with good restaurants, but its main boast is the magnificent **castle.**

It is one of Ireland's oldest, with a romantic medieval outline that has changed little in its 800 years, but the interior has been transformed over the centuries, and now contains superb Irish furniture and paintings, including a historic portrait collection which is, in effect, a National Portrait Gallery.

➕ 10A

### Malahide Castle

☎ 01-8462184 🕐 Apr–Sep Mon–Sat 10–5, Sun and public hols 10–6; Oct–Mar Mon–Sat 10–5, Sun and public hols 11–5 💰 Moderate 🍴 Restaurant (€€) 🚌 42 from Dublin 🚊 DART Malahide

## MONASTERBOICE

One of Ireland's best-known Christian sites, Monasterboice was founded by St Buite in the 6th century and thrived for 600 years, until the new Cistercian Mellifont Abbey superceded it in importance. The site includes a remarkable 10th-century round tower which stands 33m (108ft) high (without its roof) and

offers a good view of the encircling ramparts. There are also three superb high crosses, of which the South Cross (Muiredach's) is the best, a 6m (19.5ft) monolith with distinctive sculptural detail of biblical scenes. The West Cross is the tallest, and has some expressive carving, but has suffered from erosion. The North Cross has a plain, modern shaft.

➕ 9B ✉ Collon 🕐 Always accessible 🍴 Forge Gallery Restaurant (€€–€€€), Collon ☎ 041-982 6267

## POWERSCOURT HOUSE AND GARDENS

Amid the wild landscape of the Wicklow Mountains
(► 102) is one of the most superb gardens in Europe.
Powerscourt Gardens were originally laid out in the
mid-17th century to complement the magnificent
Powerscourt House. Great formal terraces step down
the south-facing slope, with distinctive mosaics of
pebbles (taken from the beach at Bray). There are
beautiful lakes and fountains, statues and decorative
ironwork, American, Italian and Japanese gardens and, in contrast,
charming kitchen gardens and a little pet's cemetery. Avid
gardeners who are inspired by all the beauty can visit the Pavilion
garden centre and take a little piece of it home.

In every direction is a backdrop of mountain peaks and Ireland's
highest waterfall plunges 121m (397ft) into a picturesque valley
within the park. The Glen of the Dargle is a wooded gorge, dotted
with modern sculpture. More than 20 years after it was destroyed
by fire, Powerscourt House reopened its doors. It houses an
exhibition about its history, which includes a visit to the former
ballroom, an excellent gallery of shops and a terrace café.

➕ 22M ✉ Enniskerry ☎ 01-2046000 🕐 Daily 9.30–5.30 (dusk in winter)
💷 Expensive 🍴 Restaurant and café (€–€€); kiosk at waterfall 🚊 DART
to Bray, then bus 185 to Enniskerry

## WEXFORD

With its huge natural harbour and its location close to the
southeastern point of Ireland, over the centuries Wexford was the
natural landing place for travellers from Wales, Cornwall and
France. The Vikings were the first settlers in the 9th or 10th
century, and the town's network of narrow lanes that cluster
behind the waterfront are a legacy of those far-off times. Wexford
was also the first Irish settlement to fall to the invading Anglo-
Normans in 1169, and soon afterwards, at Selskar Abbey, the
Anglo-Irish treaty was signed.

Wexford is an interesting mixture of working county town, with busy streets, lively pubs and a famous opera festival, and historic Heritage Town, with some of its 14th-century town wall still intact. The four-storey West Gate houses the Heritage Centre, with an audiovisual presentation about the town.

The nearby mudflats known as The Slobs are now the **Wexford Wildfowl Reserve,** with a research station, a visitor centre, hides (camouflaged shelters) and a lookout tower. The reserve is of international importance, having one-third of the world's population of Greenland white-fronted geese.

Close by is Johnstown Castle, home of the **Irish Agricultural Museum,** housed in historic farm buildings.

✚ 21J

### Irish Agricultural Museum

✉ Johnstown Castle ☎ 053-42888 🕐 Jun–Aug Mon–Fri 9–5, Sat–Sun and public hols 11–5; Mar–May, Sep–Nov, Mon–Fri 9–12.30, 1.30–5, Sat–Sun and public hols 2–5 ✋ Moderate 🍴 Coffee shop, Jul–Aug (€)

# a drive

# around the Wicklow Mountains

**This drive includes the beautiful Wicklow Mountains, two of Ireland's finest gardens and the monastic remains at Glendalough.**

*Leave Wicklow on the Dublin road and continue to Ashford.*

Mount Usher Gardens, off to the right along the banks of the River Vartry, are a superb example of 'wild gardens'.

*In Ashford turn left, then fork right, following signs for 'Roundwood'. At the T-junction by Roundwood church, turn left, then fork right, signposted 'Enniskerry'. Continue, following signs for Enniskerry.*

The entrance to Powerscourt House and Gardens is on a bend at the beginning of the village. The gardens here are among the finest in Europe, and Powerscourt Waterfall is Ireland's highest.

*In Enniskerry, turn left, and after 8km (5 miles) reach Glencree. At the next junction head for 'Sally*

*Gap, Glendalough'. After another 8km (5 miles) turn right, and keep following signs for 'Blessington' until reaching the N81. Turn left. After 3km (2 miles) turn left on to the R758 signposted 'Valleymount, Lake Drive'. Continue, following signs for Glendalough.*

This interesting ancient settlement is one of Ireland's major attractions, with atmospheric ruins.

*Return to the junction and go on through Laragh. After 5km (3 miles) turn right, signposted 'Arklow, Rathdrum R755'. In Rathdrum follow signs for 'Avoca'. At the T-junction, turn left, then bear right, signposted 'Dublin'. After 13km (8 miles) turn right to return to Wicklow.*

**Distance** 117km (73 miles)
**Time** About 5–6 hours, depending on attractions visited
**Start/end point** Wicklow ✚ 22L
**Lunch** Powerscourt Terrace Café (€)
✉ Powerscourt House
☎ 01-2046070

## THE WICKLOW MOUNTAINS

Just a short distance from the centre of Dublin (➤ 82–89) is this wonderfully secluded area of high mountains and peaceful valleys. Lugnaquilla is the highest point, at 943m (3,094ft), and is the source of the River Slaney. Two scenic passes cross the mountains from east to west – the Sally Gap on the old Military Road and the Wicklow Gap further south.

Great forests clothe many of the mountain slopes, including Coollatin Park near Shillelagh, in the south, which preserves remnants of the oak forests which are said to have supplied the roof timbers for Dublin's St Patrick's Cathedral and London's Palace of Westminster. Near Blessington is the great Poulaphouca Reservoir, providing Dublin with both water and electricity, with scenic lakeside drives and waterbus cruises.

Signs of historic habitation include ancient hillforts and stone circles, the monastic site at Glendalough (➤ 92–93) and the mansions of Powerscourt at Eniskerry (➤ 98) and Russborough House, near Blessington. More sinister associations are attached to the creepy ruin of the Hell Fire Club on top of Mount Pelier near Tallaght. Ask the locals to tell you its story, then climb up (in daylight!) for a look. The views are wonderful.

✚ 21L 🍴 Johnnie Fox's, Glencullen (€–€€) ☎ 01-2955647

## HOTELS

### AVOCA, CO WICKLOW
**Sheepwalk House (€)**
A cosy 18th-century house 3km (2 miles) from Avoca with lovely views over the Arklow Valley.
✉ Beech Road, Avoca ☎ 0402-35189; www.sheepwalk.com ⏰ Closed Dec–Jan

### DUBLIN, CO DUBLIN
**Charleville Lodge (€–€€)**
This highly recommended guesthouse is in a Victorian terrace near Phoenix Park.
✉ 268–272 North Circular Road ☎ 01-8386633; www.charlevillelodge.ie
⏰ Closed 21–26 Dec

**Harding (€)**
Good value hotel close to Temple Bar and Christ Church Cathedral. Furnishings are bright and cheerful and the bar and restaurant have music some evenings. ✉ Copper Alley, Fishamble Street
☎ 01-6796500; www.hardinghotel.ie

**Kilronian House (€€)**
Stylish Georgian house in a peaceful location close to the National Concert Hall.
✉ 70 Adelaide Road ☎ 01 475 5266; www.dublinn.com

**Merrion (€€€)**
The epitome of relaxed grandeur, the Merrion, comprising four gracious Georgian town houses, has superb bedrooms and opulent bathrooms that reflect the 18th-century architecture.
✉ Upper Merrion Street ☎ 01603 0600; www.merrionhotel.com

**Park Inn (€€€)**
In revitalized Smithfield Village, this luxurious hotel, originally called Chief O'Neill's, is dedicated to the memory of Francis O'Neill, Chicago chief of police and collector of Irish traditional music.
✉ Smithfield Village ☎ 01-8173838; www.chiefoneills.com

## KILKENNY, CO KILKENNY
### Butler House (€€–€€€)
Georgian mansion with elegant interiors, restored by the Irish
State Design Agency. Peaceful location, but close enough to the
city centre and castle to be a good base for sightseeing.
✉ 16 Patrick Street ☎ 056-7765707; www.butler.ie 🕐 Closed 24–29 Dec

## RATHNEW, CO WICKLOW
### Hunters Hotel (€€)
Rambling 16th-century coaching inn has loads of character and
lovely gardens running down to the river. Good restaurant
featuring some excellent fish dishes.
✉ Newrath Bridge ☎ 0404-40106; www.hunters.ie

### Tinakilly Country House (€€–€€€)
This elegant mansion is set in 3ha (7.5 acres), with sea views.
☎ 0404-69274; www.tinakilly.ie

## STRAFFAN, CO KILDARE
### Kildare Hotel and Country Club (€€€)
Sheer luxury and excellent food in magnificent surroundings.
Facilities include a golf course and private fishing.
☎ 01-6017200; www.kclub.ie

# RESTAURANTS

## DALKEY, CO DUBLIN
### Guinea Pig (The Fish Restaurant) (€€€€)
Family-run restaurant, adorned with rustic brass ornaments and
decorative plates, with an extensive, though not exclusively,
seafood-based menu.
✉ 17 Railway Road, Dalkey ☎ 01-2859055 🕐 Dinner only

## DUBLIN, CO DUBLIN
### Café Mao (€€)
Fashionable eatery with a slick interior serving delicious stir fries
and oriental dishes such as Malaysian chicken.
✉ 2–3 Chatham Row ☎ 01-6704899 🕐 Lunch, dinner

### Elephant and Castle (€)
Buzzy, youthful café-restaurant that was one of Temple Bar's
first new-wave places and is still one of the best. Good, generous
salads, pasta dishes and home-made burgers. Friendly, but rather
slow service.

✉ 18 Temple Bar ☎ 01-679 3121 🕐 Lunch, dinner

### Il Baccaro (€€)
Intimate Italian restaurant set in a lovely 17th-century cellar in the
heart of Temple Bar.

✉ Diceman's Corner ☎ 01671 4597 🕐 Lunch (Fri–Sun), dinner

### Kelly & Ping (€€)
A blend of Irish (the bar) and Far Eastern (the food) in the
northside's new cultural heartland. Extensive menu of interesting
dishes.

✉ Smithfield Village ☎ 01-8173840 🕐 Lunch and dinner Mon–Fri, Sat
dinner only

### Patrick Guilbaud (€€€)
See page 59.

### Queen of Tarts (€)
Super homemade cakes and pastries. Salads and cream teas, too.
All served in intimate surroundings by friendly staff.

✉ 4 Cork Hill, Dame Street ☎ 01-6707499 🕐 Daily

### Thai Orchid (€€)
Delicious Thai food and courteous service from Thai staff in
traditional costume.

✉ 7 Westmoreland Street ☎ 01-6719969 🕐 Lunch Mon–Fri; dinner daily

## ENNISKERRY, CO WICKLOW
### Powerscourt Terrace Café (€)
Wonderful views over the Powerscourt gardens and to the
mountains beyond.

✉ Powerscourt House ☎ 01-2046070 🕐 Lunch only

## GLENCULLEN, CO DUBLIN
### Johnnie Fox's Pub (€)
An 18th-century coaching inn, complete with beams and open fires, known for its excellent seafood, with fresh mussels a speciality. Music and dancing nightly.

✉ Dublin Mountains ☎ 01-2955647 🕐 Lunch, dinner; closed Sun lunch, Good Fri and 25 Dec

## GREYSTONES, CO WICKLOW
### Hungry Monk (€€)
The place for a romantic candlelit supper overlooking a scenic golf course. Good traditional Irish dishes.

✉ Church Road ☎ 01-2875759 Dinner Wed–Sat, lunch Sun only

## HOWTH, CO DUBLIN
### King Sitric Fish Restaurant (€€€)
Co Dublin's best-known fish restaurant.

✉ East Pier ☎ 01-8325235 🕐 Lunch Mon–Fri, dinner Mon–Sat; closed Sun

## KILDARE, CO KILDARE
### Silken Thomas (€–€€)
Victorian-style restaurant and bars in the centre of town with an international menu.

✉ The Square ☎ 045-521264 🕐 Lunch, dinner

## KILKENNY, CO KILKENNY
### Kilkenny Design Centre (€)
The restaurant at this complex of craft workshops matches up to the quality Irish craft wares on sale. Traditional Irish dishes and vegetarian selections.

✉ Castle Yard ☎ 056-7722118 🕐 Daily during shopping hours

## KILMACANOGE, CO WICKLOW
### Avoca Handweavers (€)
Set in the Wicklow Mountains and serving delicious home-cooked food. Good selection for vegetarians.

✉ Kilmacanoge ☎ 01-2867466 🕐 Mon–Sat 9.30–5.30, Sun 10–6

### LEIGHLINBRIDGE, CO CARLOW
**The Lord Bagenal Inn (€€)**
Country pub serving international and Irish cuisine.
✉ Main Street ☎ 059-9721668 🕓 Lunch, dinner 12–6. Bar meals Mon–Sat
9am–10pm, Sun 9–9

### MALAHIDE, CO DUBLIN
**Bon Appetit (€€€)**
There is a first-class wine list to accompany the international menu
with seafood specialities.
✉ 9 James Terrace ☎ 01-8450314 🕓 Lunch, dinner; closed Sun and public
hols, Sat lunch

### ROUNDWOOD, CO WICKLOW
**Roundwood Inn (€€)**
Cosy pub offering seafood, game and traditional Irish dishes.
✉ Roundwood ☎ 01-2818107 🕓 Restaurant: lunch Sun only, dinner
Fri–Sun. Pub food daily, all day

### WEXFORD, CO WEXFORD
**The Wrens Nest (€)**
A great place to meet the locals. Good bar meals.
✉ Custom House Quay ☎ 053-22359 🕓 Lunch Mon–Sat until 3pm

## SHOPPING

### DEPARTMENT STORES
There are large malls at Blackrock (a short walk from DART
Blackrock station), Blanchardstown (north on the N3) and the
Liffey Valley Centre (west off the N4 just beyond the M50
interchange).

The Square Towncentre at Tallaght, south of Dublin, is a superb
modern shopping centre, the largest in Ireland, with nearly 150
shops under a huge dome of natural light. Trees and shrubs thrive
in these conditions, creating an illusion of the outdoors, where
it never rains. The centre, open every day, also includes a
multiscreen cinema, restaurants, a free crèche (day nursery) and
free parking for 3,000 cars.

### Arnotts
A major refurbishment has put this store at the forefront of the new-look northside.
✉ 12 Henry Street, Dublin, Co Dublin ☎ 01-8050400 🕐 Mon–Sat 9–6.30 (to 9.30pm Thu), Sun 12–6

### Brown Thomas
Sophisticated store, with top quality goods, including designer fashions, cosmetics and china. Cafés and a hair salon.
✉ 88–92 Grafton Street, Dublin, Co Dublin ☎ 01-6056666 🕐 Mon–Sat 9–8 (to 9 Thu), Sun 10–7

### Clery's
Ireland's only remaining Irish-owned department store; as well as all the usual things, it is good for souvenirs.
✉ O'Connell Street, Dublin, Co Dublin ☎ 01-8786000 🕐 Mon–Sat 9–6.30 (to 9pm Thu, 8pm Fri), Sun 12–6

## CRAFTS
### Avoca Handweavers
The oldest working woollen mill in Ireland. All kinds of Irish-made crafts. Tea room.
✉ Avoca, Co Wicklow ☎ 01-2867466 🕐 Daily 9.30–5.30

### Carving Bogwood Sculpture
Beautiful sculptures; video and photographs tell the story of the 5,000-year-old bogwood.
✉ Barley Harbour, Newtowncashel, Co Longford ☎ 043-25297 🕐 Mon–Sat 9–6

### Cleo
Clothes made from natural fibres of Irish origin.
✉ 18 Kildare Street, Dublin, Co Dublin ☎ 01-6761421 🕐 Mon–Sat 9–5.30

### Design Yard
Features some of the best contemporary Irish craft workers and innovative artists working in glass, metal, ceramic and wood.

✉ Cow's Lane, Temple Bar, Dublin, Co Dublin ☎ 01-4741011 🕓 Daily 10–5.30

## Kilkenny Design Centre

Made in Ireland is the key here. Large selection of pottery, jewellery, glassware and fashion items. Traditional but with a touch of new creativity.

✉ 6–10 Nassau Street, Dublin, Co Dublin ☎ 01-6777066 🕓 Mon–Sat 8.30–7, Sun 11–6

## Kilkenny Design Centre

Superb range of top quality crafts from all over Ireland.

✉ Castle Yard, Kilkenny, Co Kilkenny ☎ 056-7722118 🕓 Mon–Sat 10–7, Sun 11–7. Closed Jan–early Apr

## TRADITIONAL MUSIC

### Celtic Note

Small, specialist Irish music store featuring everything from folk and traditional ballads to rock and contemporary.

✉ 12 Nassau Street, Dublin, Co Dublin ☎ 01-6704157

### Claddagh Records

A treasure trove of CDs and tapes ranging from Irish dance to traditional and modern.

✉ Cecelia Street, Temple Bar, Dublin, Co Dublin ☎ 01677 0262

# ENTERTAINMENT

## LIVE MUSIC

### Johnnie Fox's

Music every day.

✉ Glencullen, Co Dublin ☎ 01-2955647

### O'Shea's Merchant

Traditional music and dancing. You'll be encouraged to dance.

✉ 12 Lower Bridge Street, Dublin, Co Dublin ☎ 01-6796793

### The Point
Vast venue in former tram depot attracts music and dance superstars.

✉ East Link Bridge, North Wall Quay, Dublin, Co Dublin ☎ 01-8366777

### Temple Bar Music Centre
A music venue that also hosts club nights, live music, dances and fashion shows.

✉ Curved Street, Dublin, Co Dublin ☎ 01-6709202

### Whelans
Famous Dublin music venue, hosting traditional Irish, rock, jazz and blues.

✉ 25 Wexford Street, Dublin, Co Dublin ☎ 01-4780766

## NIGHTCLUBS
### Club M
✉ Blooms Hotel, 6 Anglesea Street, Dublin, Co Dublin ☎ 01-6715622

### Lillie's Bordello
✉ Adam Court, Grafton Street, Dublin, Co Dublin ☎ 01-6799204

### POD
✉ 35 Harcourt Street, Dublin, Co Dublin ☎ 01-4780225

## THEATRES AND CINEMAS
### Abbey Theatre
✉ 26 Abbey Street, Dublin, Co Dublin ☎ 01-8787222

### Gaiety Theatre
✉ South King Street, Dublin, Co Dublin ☎ 01-6771717

### Gate Theatre
✉ 1 Cavendish Row, Parnell Square, Dublin, Co Dublin ☎ 01-8744045

### Irish Film Institute
✉ 6 Eustace Street, Temple Bar, Dublin, Co Dublin ☎ 01-6795744

# The South

**A great many visitors to Ireland head straight for this southwestern corner and miss the rest of the country – which is a shame. Here you will find the great fjord-like bays which cut into the rocky west coast, between the magnificent peninsulas of An Daingean (The Dingle), the Iveragh (better known as The Ring of Kerry), the Beara and the smaller, but no less beautiful Sheep's Head and Mizen peninsulas.**

The south coast is less spectacular, but has some wonderful beaches, fine resorts and charming fishing villages such as Kinsale. Aim to be hungry when you visit here – the village is known as the Gourmet Capital of Ireland.

The southwest is not all coast and scenery. Ireland's second city, Cork, and its third, Limerick, are in this area, while towards the east are the historic city of Waterford, the great Rock of Cashel and the ancient towns and castles along the River Suir.

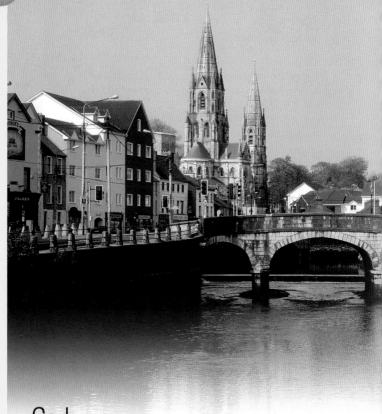

# Cork

Cork is the Republic's second largest city. At its heart is the wide St Patrick's Street, with lots of lanes leading off that are a delight to explore. Cork is a friendly city, where tradition and modern life blend easily together. It has a vibrant arts and cultural scene and was designated the European Capital of Culture for 2005.

The name Cork comes from the Irish word 'Corcaigh', meaning marsh. The older part of the city is on an island in the River Lee. From this island a network of streets branches out, giving a blend of broad malls and narrow lanes, spires, Georgian houses, busy markets and bridges that make up Cork's most prevalent features. The Lee flows into the deep waters of Cork Harbour, and this harbour brought much of the city's prosperity over the centuries. It also brought the Vikings in AD820 and later the Anglo-Normans. Cork suffered at the hands of William of Orange in 1690 and of the 'Black and Tans' (a British military force) in the 20th century. Having risen to all these challenges, Cork remains a city of unique character.

✚ 17H

ℹ Grand Parade (☎ 021-4255100)

## CORK BUTTER MUSEUM

Butter seems an odd subject for a museum, until you discover that Shandon's Butter Exchange was the largest butter market in the world, attracting customers from distant continents, and that its brand was internationally recognized as a symbol of top quality.

**www.**corkbutter.museum

✉ O'Connell Square, Shandon ☎ 021-4300600 🕒 Mar–Oct daily 10–1, 2–5 ✋ Inexpensive 🚌 3 from city centre

## CORK CITY GAOL

The thought of going to prison, if only for the afternoon, may not appeal, but Cork's former gaol is now a museum that re-creates prison life in the 19th century in an entertaining way, and also presents a good social history of the city. The former Governor's House houses the Radio Museum Experience, incorporating a 1927 studio and the RTE Museum Collection.

✉ Sunday's Well ☎ 021-4305022 🕒 Mar–Oct daily 9.30–5; Nov–Feb daily 10–4 ✋ Moderate 🍴 Coffee shop (€)

## CORK PUBLIC MUSEUM

Few city museums have such a lovely setting as this. There are 7.5ha (18.5 acres) of beautiful parkland surrounding the Georgian House which displays a wide range of collections illustrating the economic and social history of Cork, along with its Civic Regalia.

✉ Fitzgerald Park, Mardyke ☎ 021-4270679 🕓 Mon–Fri 11–1, 2.15–5 (to 6pm Jan–Aug), Sat 11–1, 2.15–4, Sun 3–5 (Apr–Sep). Closed Sun and public hols ♿ Free

## CRAWFORD ART GALLERY

Already one of Ireland's finest art galleries, the Crawford now has a wonderful new extension. Above a new glass frontage on Half Moon Street, the gallery wall swoops out over the pavement like the hull of a ship, to reflect Cork's maritime heritage. The theme continues inside, in the three curving ceiling sections above the new upper galleries, that are flooded with natural light. The lower gallery has a more restrained environment. The next phase of the Crawford Development Plan is to improve the historic original building and the grounds. As well as its permanent collection of works by Irish artists, the gallery has a lively programme of temporary exhibitions.

✉ Emmet Place ☎ 021-4273377 🕓 Mon–Sat 10–5. Closed 25 Dec–1 Jan, Sun and public hols ♿ Free 🍴 Crawford Gallery Restaurant (€€) 🚌 All city buses 🚉 Cork (10-min walk)

## ST ANNE'S CHURCH

The tall square tower of St Anne's church, capped by a gilded weather vane in the shape of a salmon, is Cork's best-known landmark. The tower is faced in red and white sandstone – the colours of Cork. Built in 1722, St Anne's is the oldest parish church still in continuous use in Cork. Its famous bells chime each quarter hour. Sunday service is at 10am.

✉ Church Street, Shandon ☎ 021-4505906 🕓 Apr–Sep daily 9–6; Oct–Mar daily 10–4 ♿ Moderate 🚌 3 from city centre

# a walk around Cork

**This walk takes in the main shopping street and the art gallery, before crossing the River Lee to Shandon, then on to the Cork Public Museum in Fitzgerald Park.**

*Walk along Grand Parade away from the statue, then bear right into St Patrick Street. At the pedestrian crossing, turn left and go along Academy Street to the Crawford Art Gallery (➤ 114).*

This fine municipal gallery has a particularly good collection of local landscapes.

*Continue round the corner and cross the bridge. Turn left, then bear right and follow signs to Shandon for the Butter Museum (▶ 113). Off the square is St Anne's Church (▶ 114).*

This Anglican Communion church is one of Cork's great landmarks, with its lofty tower and famous bells.

*Continue, passing the Shandon Arms on the left, and at the end go straight along Chapel Street.*

Opposite the end of Chapel Street is the Cathedral of St Mary and St Ann, with a beautiful, bright interior and some interesting monuments.

*Turn left along Cathedral Street, then left down Shandon Street to the river. Turn right to walk along the nearside riverbank, then at the end cross a footbridge. Follow the riverside wall then go forward between Mercy Hospital and Lee Maltings. At the end turn right and walk along Dyke Parade until you reach the gates to Fitzgerald Park on the right. The Cork Public Museum is just inside the gates (▶ 114).*

**Distance** About 2.5km (1.5 miles)
**Time** About 3 hours
**Start point** Grand Parade 🚌 All city centre buses
**End point** Fitzgerald Park 🚌 8 to city centre
**Lunch** Bells Bar and Bistro (€–€€) ✉ Quality Shandon Court Hotel, Shandon ☎ 021-4551793

# What to See in the South

## BANTRY

This lovely little town, at the head of the beautiful Bantry Bay, is a busy fishing port, its harbour overlooked by a statue of that intrepid Irish seafarer, St Brendan. Close by is the entrance to **Bantry House,** an exquisite Georgian mansion. The elegant interior contains a fine collection of furniture, Pompeiian mosaics and tapestries. The beautiful Italianate gardens have a wonderful view over the bay and delicate plants thrive in the mild climate.

✚ 15G

**Bantry House**

☎ 027-50047 🕐 Mar–Oct daily 9–6
✋ Expensive 🍴 Coffee shop (€) 🚌 Cork–Bantry bus

## THE BEARA PENINSULA

Less well known than the Ring of Kerry and The Dingle, The Beara Peninsula is just as beautiful, with its rocky, indented coastline and offshore islands. The Caha Mountains and the Slieve Miskish Mountains form its spine, creating a dramatic inland landscape, and the Healy Pass, which zig-zags across the Caha range, has wonderful views (➤ 124).

The **Sub-Tropical Gardens** on Garinish Island, in a sheltered inlet of Bantry Bay, reached by ferry from Glengarriff, is the Beara's main attraction. It is a magnificent Italian garden, with a world-famous collection of plants, which thrive here because of the warming effect of the Gulf Stream.

✚ 14H
**Sub-Tropical Gardens**
✉ Garinish Island, off Glengarriff ☎ 027-63040 🕐 Jul–Aug Mon–Sat
9.30–6.30, Sun 11–6.30; Apr–Jun, Sep Mon–Sat 10–6.30, Sun 11–6.30; Mar,
Oct Mon–Sat 10–4.30, Sun 1–5 💷 Moderate 🚌 Glengarriff main street;
Kenmare–Bantry bus passes through Glengarriff 🚢 Glengarriff main street
(separate charge for ferry)

## BLARNEY CASTLE

The 'gift of the Blarney' is known all over the world and this is
where you get it. By leaning backwards over a sheer drop
(protected by railings) from the castle battlements and kissing a
particular piece of rock, any visitor can go home endowed with a
new eloquence. The Blarney Stone is reached by ancient stone
spiral staircases through the ruins of the 15th-century castle,
which would be well worth a visit even without its notoriety.
The castle is set in lovely grounds, and is one of Ireland's most
visited places.
**www.**blarneycastle.ie
✚ 17H ✉ Blarney, Co Cork ☎ 021-4385210 🕐 Jun–Aug daily 9–7; May,
Sep daily 9–6.30; daily 9–dusk rest of year 💷 Expensive

## CASHEL

The town tends to be overshadowed by the great Rock of Cashel
(► 52–53) which dominates the skyline, but as one of Ireland's
Heritage Towns, it is well worth a visit in its own right. A good
place to start is City Hall, which has historical and folklore displays
relating to the town. There is also a **Folk Village,** with a series of
18th- to 20th-century house fronts, shops and memorabilia, and
the **Brù Borù Heritage Centre,** which offers a cultural experience
through its folk theatre, evening banquets, exhibitions and
traditional music sessions. Added in 2001, 'The Sounds of History'

exhibition is located in a subterranean setting where Ireland's musical heritage is reactivated and enhanced.

➕ 18K 🚌 Dublin–Cork buses 🚉 Thurles 18km (11 miles)

**Folk Village**

✉ Dominic Street ☎ 062-62525 🕐 Daily 9.30–7.30 (to 6pm in winter) ✋ Moderate

**Brù Borù Heritage Centre**

☎ 062-61122 🕐 Mid-Jun to mid-Sep daily 9am–11pm, shows Tue–Sat 9pm; mid-Sep to mid-Jun, Mon–Fri 9–1, 2–5, no shows ✋ Exhibition moderate; show expensive 🍴 Self-service restaurant (€). Combined evening meal and show (€€)

## CORCA DHUIBHNE (THE DINGLE PENINSULA)

See pages 40–41.

## KENMARE

Kenmare's location at the head of Kenmare Bay, surrounded by majestic mountains, earns the town its Irish name 'Neidin' or little nest. Ireland's first planned town was designed by William Petty in 1670. Today, traditional pubs, craft shops and art galleries combine well with first-class hotels, guesthouses and award-winning restaurants. The Heritage Centre explains the history of Kenmare using personal audiotours and exhibitions include exhibits on Kenmare lace and the Nun of Kenmare.

➕ 15H 🍴 P F McCarthy's, Main Street (€€)

ℹ Tourist Information (☎ 064-41233)

## THE RING OF KERRY

The road which encircles the Iveragh peninsula is popularly known as the Ring of Kerry, an exceptionally scenic circular

route of 107km (66 miles) if you start and finish in Killarney. From here you go south through the national park to Kenmare, then strike out along the north shore of the Kenmare estuary, through the lovely resort of Parknasilla. The famous Great Southern Hotel here has played host to the rich and famous for many years.

Farther along is Caherdaniel. The route heads north from here around Ballinskelligs Bay to Waterville, then on to Cahersiveen, the 'capital' of the peninsula and birthplace of the politician Daniel O'Connell. It also has an interesting Heritage Centre. The road then heads eastwards, with Dingle Bay to the north, through Killorglin, a market town famous for its Puck Fair in August, then back to Killarney.

As if the wonderful coast and mountain scenery were not enough, the peninsula is also blessed with a warm Gulf Stream climate.

✚ 14H 🍴 Blind Piper Bar Restaurant (€–€€), Caherdaniel
ℹ Killarny Tourist Information (☎ 064-31633)

## KILLARNEY

Killarney is one of the busiest tourist towns in Ireland, not for its own attractions so much as for its surroundings.

Although it has many pubs and shops, it is essentially a base for exploring the beauties of Kerry, and is the traditional starting point for the Ring of Kerry. The Killarney National Park, 10,000ha (24,710 acres) of beautiful mountains, woodland and lakes, is right on the doorstep, and is the setting for Muckross House (➤ 46–47).

Jarveys are the drivers of the horse-drawn jaunting cars you will see lined up along the roadside in Killarney. Haggling over the fee is an acceptable part of the deal, but remember that you are not just paying to get from A to B – jarveys are an intrinsic part of the Killarney experience and will usually spin a yarn or two along the way.

✚ 15J

# around Kerry and Cork

**This drive includes the wonderful wooded mountains of the Killarney National Park, the spectacular Healy Pass and two of Ireland's finest historic houses.**

*From Killarney take the N71, signposted to Muckross, and soon reach the Killarney National Park and Muckross House (▶ 46–47).*

Muckross' location amid the mountains and lakes of the national park is unsurpassed.

*Continue on the N71, passing Torc Waterfall, to reach Ladies' View, then after 6km (4 miles), at Molls Gap, bear left, signposted to Kenmare, Glengarriff. At Kenmare drive up the main street and turn right, then leave the town following signs for Glengarriff and Bantry. Cross a river bridge and turn right, signposted Castletown Bearhaven R571. Continue for about 14km (22.5 miles) then follow signs for Healy Pass.*

This pass across the Caha Mountains has stunning views and a breathtaking summit.

*Over the top of the pass, descend a series of hairpin bends and continue to reach a T-junction. Turn left for Glengarriff or right to lunch in Castletownbere.*

Garinish Island, with its beautiful sub-tropical gardens, can be reached by ferry from Glengarriff.

*Continue for 5.6km (3.5 miles) to Bantry.*

By the harbour on the Cork road is Bantry House (➤ 118) and the Armada Exhibition.

*Retrace the route to Glengarriff, then take the N71 to Kenmare and Killarney.*

**Distance** 140km (67 miles)
**Time** 6–7 hours depending on attractions visited
**Start/end point** Killarney ✚ 15J
**Lunch** The Copper Kettle (€) ✉ The Square, Castletownbere
☎ 027-71792 ◷ Mon–Sat

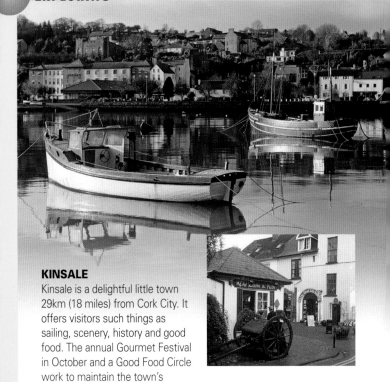

## KINSALE

Kinsale is a delightful little town 29km (18 miles) from Cork City. It offers visitors such things as sailing, scenery, history and good food. The annual Gourmet Festival in October and a Good Food Circle work to maintain the town's famously high culinary standards. Historically, Kinsale is remembered for the 1601 battle, when a Spanish fleet came to aid Hugh O'Neill's struggle against the English. The Irish/Spanish force were defeated, thus marking the decline of the old Gaelic order, with the 'Flight of the Earls' to Europe. The late 17th-century Charles Fort at Summercove is open to visitors, while James Fort is in ruins but is still worth a visit for the grand views of the town and harbour. It was off this coast that the *Lusitania* was sunk by a German submarine in 1915, with the loss of 1,500 lives. Places of interest to visit in Kinsale are the Courthouse, *c*1600, which now houses a regional museum

✚ 17G 🍴 Fishy Fishy (€–€€), Guardwell (☎ 021-4774453)

ℹ Tourist Information (☎ 021-4772234)

## LIMERICK

The Republic's third largest city, Limerick is a cultural centre, well endowed with theatres, art galleries and museums – notably the **Hunt Museum.** Located in the elegant 18th-century Custom House, the gallery has one of the greatest private collections of art and antiquities in the country.

The River Shannon flows through the city, overlooked by **King John's Castle** and crossed by many fine bridges. The oldest part of the city is on King's Island, first settled by the Vikings, and it is here that the most important historical sites are found, including the castle and the 12th-century Protestant cathedral.

The city's architecture is jealously guarded by the Limerick Civic Trust. The best old street is The Crescent, while examples of modern architecture are the Civic Centre and City Hall on Merchant's Quay.

➕ 17K

**Hunt Museum**

✉ Custom House, Rutland Street ☎ 061-312833; www.huntmuseum.com
🕐 Mon–Sat 10–5, Sun 2–5 🍴 Restaurant (€€) ✋ Expensive
🚌 All city centre buses

**King John's Castle**

➕ Nicholas Street, King's Island ☎ 061-360788 🕐 Apr–Oct daily 10–5.30; Nov–Mar daily 10.30–4.30 ✋ Expensive

## MUCKROSS HOUSE

See pages 46–47.

## ROCK OF CASHEL

See pages 52–53.

## WATERFORD

Waterford grew from an ancient Viking settlement into the foremost port in Ireland, and its quays are still busy with international trade; the famous **Waterford Crystal Visitor Centre** reflects this. The city preserves an atmosphere of the past, and the mixture of Celt, Viking, Norman, English, Flemish and Huguenot gives a European flavour which is reflected on the sea front and in its narrow lanes. One of the oldest buildings is Reginald's Tower, built by the Vikings in 1003, which now houses the city museum. The Church of Ireland cathedral is regarded as the finest 18th-century ecclesiastical building in Ireland, and the Catholic cathedral has a wonderful interior, with superb carving and stained glass.

✚ 20J

### Waterford Crystal Visitor Centre

✉ Kilbarry ☎ 051-332500 🕐 Visitor centre and shop: Mar–Oct daily 9–6; Nov–Feb daily 9–5. Tours: Mar–Oct daily 9–4.15, Nov–Feb Mon–Fri 9–3.15
✋ Expensive 🍴 Restaurant (€–€€) 🚌 Waterford–Ballybeg

## HOTELS

### ADARE, CO LIMERICK
**Adare Manor (€€€)**
An opulent hotel in a Gothic mansion, surrounded by parkland beside the River Maigue; including a championship golf course and other leisure facilities.
✉ On Limerick to Tralee route ☎ 061-396566; www.adaremanor.com

### CLONAKILTY, CO CORK
**Inchydoney Island Lodge & Spa (€€€)**
Modern coastal hotel in blue flag beach setting. Home to Ireland's only thalassotherapy (seawater) spa.
✉ Clonakilty, West Cork ☎ 023-33143; www.inchydoneyisland.com

### CORK, CO CORK
**Isaacs Hotel (€€)**
One of Cork's finest hotels, with good accommodation and the celebrated Greenes Restaurant.
✉ 48 MacCurtain Street ☎ 021-4503805; www.isaccs.ie

### KENMARE, CO KERRY
**Brooklane Hotel (€€)**
This new hotel offers friendly, personal service. Casey's restaurant has good food and Irish music and the Cinnamon Club hosts top Irish music artists.
✉ Gortamullen, Kenmare ☎ 064-42077; www.brooklane.com

**Park Hotel (€€€)**
Country house hotel overlooking Kenmare Bay and home to the deluxe spa 'Samas'.
✉ On the R569 ☎ 064-41200; www.parkkenmare.com 🕒 Closed 4 Jan to 10 Apr

### KILLARNEY, CO KERRY
**Aghadoe Heights (€€€)**
In a superb setting high above the Killarney Lakes, this hotel offers luxury and hospitality and an excellent restaurant.

✉ 5km (3 miles) north of Killarney off N22 Tralee road ☎ 064-31766; www.aghadoeheights.com ⏰ Check for winter closure

## KINSALE, CO CORK
### Deasy's Long Quay House (€€)
Splendid Georgian residence overlooking the inner harbour and yacht marina.

✉ Long Quay ☎ 021-4774563; www.longquayhousekinsale.com ⏰ Closed Nov, Dec

## LIMERICK, CO LIMERICK
### Best Western Pery's Hotel (€€)
This historic city centre hotel is in the heart of Georgian Limerick, and is perfect for shopping and restaurants.

✉ Glentworth Street ☎ 061-413822; www.perys.ie

## WATERFORD, CO WATERFORD
### Waterford Castle & Golf Club (€€€)
A real castle on an island with many of its original features, including 16th-century oak panelling, stone walls and graceful arches, and modern leisure facilities including adjacent 18-hole, par 72 championship golf course.

✉ The Island, Ballinakill ☎ 051-878203; www.waterfordcastle.com

## RESTAURANTS

### BALLINGARRY, CO LIMERICK
### The Mustard Seed (€€€)
A pleasant drive through the Limerick countryside on quiet lanes leads to this first-class restaurant in a stylish country house. Also offers B&B.

✉ Echo Lodge ☎ 069-68508 ⏰ Dinner only; closed 24–26 Dec

### BALTIMORE, CO CORK
### Chez Youen (€€–€€€)
Among the best fish restaurants in Ireland.

✉ The Square ☎ 028-20136 ⏰ Lunch Sun only, dinner daily in summer, Thu–Sat in winter

## BANTRY, CO CORK
### O'Connor's Seafood Restaurant (€–€€)
Fresh local fish and shellfish are the specialities here.

⊠ The Square ☎ 027-50221 ⏰ Lunch, dinner

## CLOGHROE, CO CORK
### Blairs Inn (€–€€)
In a secluded riverside setting near Blarney. Good Irish cuisine, including fish, duck, steaks and game, all from local sources. Traditional music Mondays (summer only).

⊠ Cloghroe, Blarney ☎ 021-4381470 ⏰ Lunch, dinner, all-day bar menu

## CORK, CO CORK
### Crawford Art Gallery (€€)
Excellent Irish and Mediterranean dishes.

⊠ Emmet Place ☎ 021-4274415 ⏰ Breakfast, lunch, afternoon tea; closed Sun

### Jacques (€€)
Well-reviewed restaurant creating modern Irish dishes from excellent local produce, including farm-reared ducks, fish and organic vegetables.

⊠ Phoenix Street ☎ 021-4277387 ⏰ Lunch Mon–Fri, dinner Mon–Sat

## DINGLE, CO KERRY
### The Charterhouse Restaurant (€–€€)
Excellent cuisine in this cosy harbourside restaurant.

⊠ The Mail Raod ☎ 066-9152255 ⏰ Dinner daily Mar–Oct; Nov–Feb Thu–Sun; closed 6 Jan–13 Feb

### Lord Baker's (€€)
Fish, game and succulent steaks are the speciality of this excellent restaurant.

⊠ Main Street ☎ 066-9151277 ⏰ Lunch, dinner; closed Thu and 24–26 Dec

## KENMARE, CO KERRY
### Packie's (€€)
Stylish but unpretentious restaurant with creative cooking; intensely flavoured Irish-Mediterranean food.
✉ Henry Street ☎ 064-41508 ◷ Dinner Tue–Sat mid-Mar to mid-Oct (Jun–Aug Mon–Sat); Oct to mid-Jan Wed–Sat

### Prego (€–€€)
Good atmosphere and tasty food in this well -priced family restaurant.
✉ Henry Street ☎ 064-42350 ◷ Lunch, dinner

## KILLARNEY, CO KERRY
### Foley's Seafood and Steak Restaurant (€€)
The name says it all, and the restaurant is famous for it.
✉ 23 High Street ☎ 064-31217 ◷ Lunch, dinner; closed 24–26 Dec and lunch in winter

### Old Presbytery Restaurant (€€)
Quality Irish ingredients well prepared in this attractive Georgian restaurant.
✉ Cathedral Place ☎ 064-30555 ◷ Mon–Sat lunch and dinner; closed Jan

## KINSALE, CO CORK
### Fishy Fishy (€)
Fresh fish, shellfish, salads and desserts feature in this popular seafood speciality eatery.
✉ Market Place ☎ 021-4774453 ◷ Daily 10–4; closed Sun Oct–Mar

### Man Friday (€€)
One of Kinsale's longest-established restaurants, with an excellent reputation for its modern Irish and international cuisine.
✉ Scilly ☎ 021-4772260 ◷ Dinner only; closed Sun (except public hols)

## LIMERICK, CO LIMERICK
### Duckarts Restaurant (€)
This museum restaurant serves good food and has lovely views of the Shannon.

✉ Hunt Museum, The Custom House, Rutland Street ☎ 061-321833
🕐 Mon–Sat 10–5, Sun 2–5

### Freddy's Bistro (€€)
This restaurant, serving Irish and continental dishes, is full of character.

✉ Theatre Lane, Lower Glentworth Street ☎ 061-418749 🕐 Dinner Tue–Sat

## NEW ROSS, CO WATERFORD
### The Galley Cruising Restaurant (€€€)
Cruising restaurants ply the waters of the rivers Barrow and Nore from New Ross and Waterford, offering a wonderfully relaxing way to eat and enjoy the scenery at the same time. The *St Ciaran* and *St Brendan* can carry 70 or 80 diners. Lunch, afternoon tea and dinner cruises are all available. reservations essential.

✉ The Quay, New Ross ☎ 051-421723; www.rivercruise.ie 🕐 Apr–Oct

## WATERFORD, CO WATERFORD
### The Wine Vault (€–€€)
A warm and cosy wine bar specializing in seafood.

✉ High Street ☎ 051-853444 🕐 Lunch, dinner; closed Sun, Good Fri and 25 Dec

## SHOPPING

### ANTIQUES
#### George Stackpole
Antiques and books, bought and sold.

✉ Main Street, Adare, Co Limerick ☎ 061-396409

#### O'Keef's Antiques
Antiquarian books, paintings, silver and more.

✉ 15 Princes Quay, Adare, Co Limerick ☎ 066-7125635

## CRAFTS
### Black Abbey Crafts
Good selection of quality Irish cafts, including ceramics, slate, iron and glass items.

✉ Adare, Co Limerick ☎ 061-396021 🕐 Mon–Sat 10–6

### Blarney Woollen Mills
First established in 1750, the company now offers woven rugs and Aran sweaters, plus crystal, china and gifts.

✉ Blarney, Co Cork ☎ 021-4516111

### Louis Mulcahy Pottery
This renowned pottery sells quality hand-painted lampshades, sculpted masks, dinner services and much more.

✉ Clogher Head, West Dingle, Co Kerry ☎ 066-9156229; www.louismulcahy.com 🕐 May–Jun daily 9–7; Jul–Aug daily 9–8; daily 9–6 rest of year

## MARKETS
### The English Market
Covered market with array of food stalls daily.

✉ Princes Street/Patrick Street/Grand Parade, Cork, Co Cork

### Milk Market
Retail outlets open all week; arts and crafts market on Friday; traditional market Saturday morning.

✉ Corn Market Row, Limerick, Co Limerick

## SHOPPING CENTRES
### Arthur's Quay Shopping Centre
Very attractive collection of over 30 stores in a prime city-centre location; restaurants, day nursery, play area and plenty of parking.

✉ Limerick, Co Limerick

### Killarney Outlet Centre
✉ Fair Hill, Killarney

### Merchant's Quay Shopping Centre
✉ 1 Patrick Street, Cork, Co Cork

## TRADITIONAL MUSIC
### Living Tradition
The music shop of Ossian Music Company. Traditional instruments, sheet music, CDs, cassettes and videos.
✉ 40 MacCurtain Street, Cork, Co Cork ☎ 021-4502040

### The Sounds of Music
Good range of CDs including traditional Irish music and a selection of instruments.
✉ Henry Street, Kenmare, Co Kerry ☎ 064-4226

### Variety Sounds
A wide range of guitars, *bodhráns*, whistles, CDs and books.
✉ 7 College Street, Killarney, Co Kerry ☎ 064-35755

## ENTERTAINMENT

## LIVE MUSIC
### Crowley's
If it's tradition you are seeking you'll find it here in the heart of Kenmare. Impromptu Irish music sessions take place regularly.
✉ Henry Street, Kenmare, Co Kerry ☎ 064-41472

### De Barra's Pub
Famous landmark pub featuring live folk and traditional music.
✉ Pearse Street, Clonakilty, Co Cork ☎ 023-33381

### Dingle An Droichead Beag
Dingle's musical centre.
✉ Main Street, Dingle, Co Kerry ☎ 066-9151723

### Lobby Bar
Traditional music of Ireland and elsewhere. Concert venue upstairs.
✉ 1 Union Quay, Cork, Co Cork ☎ 021-4311113

## The Old Oak Bar
Top music venue in Cork. Live bands and traditional sessions on two floors.

✉ 113 Oliver Plunkett Street, Cork, Co Cork ☎ 0121-4276165

## The Warehouse
Live music venue, located behind a pub which has traditional music and dancing.

✉ Behind Dolan's Pub, Alphonsus Street, off Dock Road, Limerick, Co Limerick ☎ 061-314483

## NIGHTCLUB
### Newport
Late-night funky lounge and adjacent nightclub.

✉ Paul Street Plaza, Cork, Co Cork ☎ 021-4254872; 021-4254874

## THEATRES AND CINEMAS
### Beltable Arts Centre
A venue for theatre, concerts, dance, mime and poetry.

✉ 69 O'Connell Street, Limedrick, Co Limerick ☎ 061-319866

### Cinemax
✉ The Quay, Limerick, Co Limerick ☎ 027-55777; www.cinemaxbantry.com

### Siamsa Tire – The National Folk Theatre of Ireland
Keeping the national traditions alive.

✉ Town Park, Tralee, Co Kerry ☎ 066-7123055

### Theatre Royal
Hosts the Opera Festival and The Waterford Show.

✉ The Mall, Waterford, Co Waterford ☎ 051-874402

### Triskal Arts Centre
Drama, readings, children's theatre and music.

✉ Tobin Street, Cork, Co Cork ☎ 021-4272022

# The West

**The wild beauty of the west is underlaid with the hostility of a landscape that does its best to defy cultivation. There are fields, but they are the size of pocket handkerchiefs, and the drystone walls that enclose them have by no means used up all of the land's loose rocks.**

Vast empty areas of blanket bog have pockets of wetness that expand into a network of lakes and rivers beneath the mountains of Connemara and Joyce's Country. The great Loughs – Conn, Mask and Corrib – lie between Sligo and Galway bays. Farther east the River Shannon forms the backbone of a watery highway. In Clare, The Burren is a moonscape of bare limestone, where plants cling on to the sparse soil, and the western boundary of all this is a jagged and spectacular coastline.

# Galway

Galway, the historic capital of Connaught, is Ireland's fourth largest city, with a delightful blend of ancient and modern. It has at its heart a maze of narrow streets, lined with a mixture of modern shop-fronts, traditional-style painted façades, old pubs and restaurants. A relaxed west-coast atmosphere prevails, enlivened by an energetic student population.

Situated in the northeast corner of Galway Bay, where the River Corrib pours into the sea, Galway was built on international trade and sea fishing, and its oldest parts cluster around the harbour and riverside quays. On the east bank is the Spanish Arch, built to protect cargoes of wine and brandy from Iberia. Behind the quay is a network of narrow streets, leading off from the main thorough-fare. A modern shopping mall, incorporating part of the medieval city wall, is hidden away behind old façades. On the far side of the river is The Claddagh, once a close-knit Gaelic-speaking fishing community and now remembered in the continuing tradition of the Claddagh ring, with two hands holding a crowned heart.

Apart from its own attractions, Galway is a good base for exploring the surrounding areas – Connemara, Lough Corrib, the Aran Islands and the Burren.

Salthill is Galway's seaside resort suburb, to the west, offering a good range of amusements and a popular long sandy beach.

**www**.irelandwest.ie

✚ 16M

ℹ Tourist Information (☎ 091-537700)

## CATHEDRAL OF OUR LADY ASSUMED INTO HEAVEN AND ST NICHOLAS

Overlooking the River Corrib near the Salmon Weir Bridge, this splendid modern Roman Catholic **cathedral** opened in 1965 and looked so grand that the locals dubbed it the 'Taj Michael', after the then Bishop of Galway, Michael (pronounced Mee-hawl) Brown.

Built on the site of the former county gaol (jail), it's topped by a great copper dome, and the interior is plain but impressive, with floors of Connemara marble, rough-hewn limestone walls and superb stained glass. It was designed by John J Robinson and replaced the old cathedral on Abbeygate Street, which has been converted into shops.

✉ University and Gaol roads ☎ 091-563577 🕐 Daily 8.30–6.30 ✋ Free (donations welcome) 🍴 Restaurant (€–€€)

## NORA BARNACLE HOUSE MUSEUM

Built around the end of the 19th century, this tiny cottage now houses one of the smallest museums in Ireland. It was formerly the home of the eponymous Nora Barnacle, companion, wife and lifelong inspiration of the writer James Joyce. He is said to have based the character of Molly Bloom in his novel *Ulysses* on her. Even without the collections of memorabilia, it is impossible to ignore the romantic associations.

✉ 8 Bowling Green ☎ 091-564743 🕐 Mid-May to mid-Sep Mon–Sat 10–5 ✋ Inexpensive

## ST NICHOLAS'S CHURCH

St Nicholas's Church is the largest medieval parish church in Ireland still in constant use. It was built around 1320 by the Lynch family and consecrated to the patron saint of sailors. Christopher Columbus worshipped here in 1477, and was no doubt inspired by tales of St Brendan the Navigator, an Irish monk who sailed to America in the 6th century. Outside the church, on the site of the former college, there is a colourful weekly Saturday market where crafts, organic vegetables and food are sold. In addition to its regular services, St Nicholas's hosts concerts throughout the year.

✉ Market Street ☎ 091-563081 🕐 Daily 11–5; check for services

# a walk around Galway

*From Eyre Square, the heart of the city, walk along William Street, Shop Street and High Street. At the cobbled crossroads keep forward along Quay Street.*

On the corner is Thomas Dillon's Claddagh Gold, a little jeweller's shop with a Claddagh Ring Museum in the back room. At the end is the famous Spanish Arch, where Iberian traders would land their cargoes, behind which is the new Galway City Museum.

*Take the riverside path that leads off between the bridge and Jury's Hotel. Cross the next road and continue alongside the river on your left, and a canal on your right. At the end of the path, cross a footbridge over the canal, then turn left and walk to the Salmon Weir Bridge. Cross the bridge and the Cathedral of Our Lady Assumed into Heaven and St Nicholas is immediately ahead.*

The Cathedral, completed in 1965, is topped by a great copper dome. The interior is light, spacious and, though plain, is still very impressive.

*Recross the bridge and turn right down Newtown Smith, passing the footbridge crossed earlier. Keep forward, turn right at the crossroads, then at the end bear left. About halfway along on the right is the Nora Barnacle House Museum.*

This tiny cottage is where the writer James Joyce courted his future wife. Mementoes of the couple are on display.

*At the end, opposite St Nicholas's Church, turn left into Market Street, then right into Upper Abbeygate Street.*

The building at the end, on the right, is Lynch's Castle, now the Allied Irish Bank.

*Turn left into William Street and return to Eyre Square.*

**Distance** About 2km (1.2 miles)
**Time** 2–3 hours
**Start/end point** Eyre Square
🚌 All city centre buses
**Lunch** McDonagh's Seafood House
(€–€€€) ✉ 22 Quay Street
☎ 091-565001 🕐 Seafood Bar:
Mon–Sat 12–9.45, Sun from 5pm
(2pm in summer). Fish and chips:
Mon–Sat 12–midnight, Sun 5–11

# What to See in the West

### BUNRATTY CASTLE AND FOLK PARK

Bunratty, 14.5km (9 miles) northeast of Limerick, is Ireland's most complete medieval castle, thanks to the superb restoration work done in 1960 when the former ruin was purchased by Bord Failte and Lord Gort. Following the restoration, Lord Gort installed his collections of furniture, *objets d'art*, paintings and tapestries, all of which predate 1650. The castle has become famous for its medieval banquets, with historic costume and traditional food and entertainment.

In the castle grounds, Irish village life at the turn of the century has been re-created, with reconstructed urban and rural dwellings, farmhouses, a watermill, forge and village street, complete with shops and a pub – all brought to life by knowledgeable costumed guides. The restored Regency walled garden opened in June 2000.

✚ 16K ⊠ N18 Bunratty ☎ 061-360788 ⏱ Daily 9–5.30, (until 6 Jun–Aug). Last admission 45 mins before closing 💷 Expensive 🍴 Tea room (€); lunches in barn May–Oct (€); Mac's Pub (€€) 🚌 From Limerick, Ennis and Galway 🚆 Limerick and Ennis

## THE BURREN AND AILLWEE CAVE

The Burren National Park preserves a remarkable landscape that continues to excite geologists and botanists from far and wide. It is a vast plateau of limestone hills which were scraped free of their soil by retreating glaciers 15,000 years ago, then eroded by rain and Atlantic mists. The tiny amounts of soil that gather in the rock fissures support both Alpine and Mediterranean plant life, and early summer is the main flowering season.

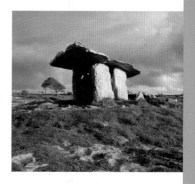

**The Burren Exposure** visitors' centre provides an overview of the area and its unique landscape, its human history and its famous flora. Aillwee Cave, south of Ballyvaughan, has fossil formations and water figures. The Burren is best appreciated on foot, and the waymarked 42km (26-mile) Burren Way, running from Ballyvaughan and Liscannor, can be undertaken in short sections.

✚ 16L

### Burren Exposure

⊠ Ballyvaughan ☎ 065-7077277 ⏱ Mar–Nov daily 9–6

### Aillwee Cave

⊠ Ballyvaughan ☎ 065-7077036 ⏱ Tours only: daily from 10am, last tour 5.30 (Jul and 6 Aug); Dec by appointment only

## CASTLEBAR

Castlebar is the county town of Co Mayo. Its most notable attraction is the new Irish folklife collection. Housed in a renovated 18th-century building, along with purpose-built extensions and grounds, this is the first branch of the National Museum to be located outside Dublin. Displays utilizing 50,000 items, reflect the lives of Ireland's people and their trades, illustrating the social history of Ireland over the past 200 years.

➕ 4B

**Museum of Country Life**

**www.**museum.ie

✉ Turlough Park House ☎ 094 9031755 🕐 Tue–Sat 10–5, Sun 2–5 🍴 Restaurant

## CLIFFS OF MOHER

These towering cliffs rise sheer out of the turbulent Atlantic to a height of nearly 213m (700ft) and stretch for 8km (5 miles) along the Clare coast north of Hag's Head. Majestic in calm weather, the cliffs are most dramatic (and dangerous) when stormy seas crash into their base, hurling pebbles high up into the air. Horizontal layers of flagstones have been exposed by coastal erosion, making convenient perches for the sea birds, including puffins, which abound here. At the highest point of the cliffs, **O'Brien's Tower** (closed for restoration until 2007) was constructed in the early 19th century as a lookout point for the first tourists, and gives views of the Clare Coastline, the Oileáin Árann (Aran Islands) and mountains as far apart as Kerry and Connemara. A new visitor centre will open in 2007.

➕ 15L

**O'Brien's Tower and Visitor Centre**

✉ Near Liscannor ☎ 065-7081565 🕐 Tower: Mar–Oct 9.30–5.30; Visitor Centre: daily 9.30–5.30 (Jun–Aug 9–7) ✋ Inexpensive; nearby parking €4 per car 🍴 Tea room (€) 🚌 From Lahinch and other nearby towns

## CLONMACNOISE
See pages 38–39.

## CONNEMARA
To the northwest of Galway City is Connemara, with some of the most dramatic scenery in Ireland. Much of its convoluted

coastline, with masses of tiny islands and some excellent beaches, can be followed by road and the views are spectacular. Inland, in southern Connemara, are thousands of lakes amid the bogland. Further north, and hardly ever out of sight, are the brooding ranges of the Twelve Pins and the Maumturk Mountains. Connemara Marble is quarried at Recess, and there is a factory shop and showroom at Connemara Marble Industries in Moycullen. The Connemara National Park protects about 2,000ha (4,940 acres) of the mountains, bogs, heaths and grasslands, and there is a good visitor centre in Letterfrack that has plenty of information – and a herd of Connemara ponies.

✚ 3A

**National Park Visitor Centre**

✉ Letterfrack ☎ 095-41054 🕓 Jul–Aug daily 9.30–6; Jul 10–6; Sep to mid-Oct, Apr–May daily 10–5.30

✋ Inexpensive 🍴 Tea rooms (€) ❓ Guided walks Jun–Aug. Talks and special events for children

# a drive around the coast, lakes and mountains of Connemara

**This drive follows the coastline for much of the way, with views of the Oileáin Árann (Aran Islands) in the early stages. It then passes through isolated settlements amid a rocky landscape, with mountain views, to end at the lovely little town of Clifden.**

*From Galway follow signs for Salthill until you reach a roundabout on the seafront, then take the Spiddal road west along Galway Bay. At the T-junction turn left, signposted Carraroe and Barna, then after about 13km (8 miles) pass through Spiddal.*

There are breathtaking views along the coast and across Galway Bay before the road swings right to open up an inland vista of distant mountains.

*Turn right on to the R336, signed 'Cill Ciarain, Scriob, Carna and Ros Muc', then after 11km (7 miles) at a T-junction, make a left turn signed 'Connemara Scenic Route'. Continue through Cill Ciarain (Kilkieran), then after 8.5km (5 miles) bear right, signed 'Clifden', with views of the Twelve Pins ahead. Turn left on to the R342 and follow signs for Roundstone.*

This charming village is the home of Malachy Kearns' bodrhán workshop, where the craftsman can often be seen making his famous traditional Irish drums. There is also a pottery close by.

*After 13km (8 miles) reach Ballyconneely and continue around the rocky bay, then turn left into Clifden after a further 9km (5.5 miles).*

If you want to complete the circle, the road back to Galway (about 48km/30 miles) is well signposted.

**Distance** 112km (70 miles)
**Time** About 5 hours, including stop for lunch and visits to craft workshops
**Start point** Galway ✚ 16M
**End point** Clifden ✚ 3A
**Lunch** O'Dowds Seafood Restaurant (€€–€€€) ✉ Roundstone
☎ 095-35809

## KNAPPOGUE CASTLE

Built in the mid-15th century for the MacNamara family, Knappogue underwent many changes over the course of the next five centuries. It was extended and adapted and used as government offices for a while, before falling into a ruinous state. In the 1960s it was acquired by Mark Edwin Andrews, then Assistant Secretary to the US Navy. He and his wife set about the task of restructuring the castle into an authentic setting for the medieval banquets which continue to be popular. They include dinner and a pageant, with stories of the history of the women of Ireland – real and legendary. The castle was acquired by the Shannon Development Company in 1996.

✚ 16L ✉ Kilmurry, near Quin ☎ 061-360788 ⏰ Apr–Oct daily 9.30–5 (last admission 1 hour before closing) ✋ Moderate ❓ Medieval banquets on demand

## KYLEMORE ABBEY

Kylemore Abbey's greatest attraction is its location. Nestled at the base of Duchruach Mountain, and on the north shores of Lough Pollacapul in the heart of the Connemara Mountains, it is regarded as one of Ireland's most romantic buildings. Lying in a rhododendron-filled hollow, this neo-Gothic estate castle was constructed for British shipping magnate and Irish politican Mitchell Henry. Since 1920 it has been a convent of the Irish Benedictine nuns, and a girls' boarding school now occupies the building. It offers the warmth and hospitality of its peaceful setting to visitors from all over the world. The restaurant has the best of home cooking and a range of the abbey's distinctive pottery can be seen in the studio. Within the grounds there is a Gothic chapel, which has a Connemara marble interior. Nearby is a *taghallai*, a pre-Christian tomb. The 2.5ha (6-acre) restored Victorian walled garden is well worth a visit, as is the visitor centre.

➕ 3A ✉ Connemara ☎ 095-41146 🕐 Visitor Centre: Mar–Nov daily 9.30–5.30. Gardens: mid-Mar to Oct daily 9.30–5.30. Closed Christmas week and Good Friday
💰 Expensive 🍴 Tearoom (€–€€) 🚌 No bus

## OILEÁIN ÁRANN (ARAN ISLAND)
See pages 50–51.

## THE SHANNON
Ireland's longest river, the Shannon rises in a humble pool (called the Shannon Pot) in Co Cavan, then gathers strength as it flows through a series of lakes before it meets the Atlantic beyond Limerick. Historically, river crossings were always points where towns grew and prospered. Places such as Carrick-on-Shannon and Athlone are bases for the leisure cruiser holidays for which this mighty river is so popular.

➕ 16K
ℹ Shannon Development (☎ 061-361555)

## SLIGO

Sligo is a lively and attractive town with splendid old shop-fronts and traditional music pubs. It is also a significant cultural centre and has a fine range of art galleries and museums, as well as the various festivals which take place throughout the year.

Over 1,000 years of history have shaped the town, but it is literature that attracts many of its visitors. This is Yeats country, and the subject of one of his best-known poems is just outside the town – the Isle of Inisfree in Lough Gill (riverboat trips to the lough depart from Sligo's Doorly Park). Sligo also has two fine cathedrals and Sligo Abbey, a Dominican friary founded in 1252.

✚ 6C

🛈 Temple Street (☎ 071-9161201)

## WESTPORT

Set on Clew Bay, Westport is one of the liveliest and most charming towns in the west of Ireland, with broad Georgian streets and a leafy riverside avenue at its heart. Nearby **Westport House** dates from the 1730s and is the only stately home open to the public in Sligo. It is beautifully furnished and has some superb Waterford crystal, silver and paintings. The dungeons are from an earlier building, reputedly a castle of Grace O'Malley, the 16th-century pirate queen, and the grounds contain many rides and amusements for children.

✚ 4B

**Westport House**

**www.**westporthouse.ie

✉ The Quay, Westport ☎ 098-25430/27766 🕐 Jul–Oct daily 11.30–5; Apr–Jun Mon, Sat–Sun 11.30–5; Nov, Sat–Sun 11.30–5 💲 Expensive
🍴 Café Jun, Aug only (€)

## YEATS TOWER, THOOR BALLYLEE

In 1917 the poet William Butler Yeats bought this derelict 16th-century tower house and renovated it. For the next 12 years he and his family spent their summers here and it was in these peaceful surroundings that he wrote most of his works. His friend and patron, Lady

Gregory, lived nearby, and together they were the inspiration behind the Irish Literary Revival and the founding of the Abbey Theatre in Dublin (➤ 110). In the 1960s Thoor Ballylee was again restored, to show how it looked when Yeats was here, and was opened to the public.

✚ 17M ✉ Gort ☎ 091-631436 (off season 091-537700) 🕐 May–Sep daily 10–6 💲 Moderate
❓ Audiovisual presentation and displays of first editions. Bookshop, craft centre, picnic area

# HOTELS

## BUNRATTY, CO CLARE
### Bunratty Woods Country House (€–€€)
Situated in the grounds of Bunratty Castle, this guesthouse contains many interesting antiques and has mountain views.
✉ Low Road ☎ 061-369689 🕒 Closed 7 Nov–early Mar

## CASHEL, CO GALWAY
### Cashel House (€€–€€€)
Gracious country house hotel in superb gardens overlooking Cashel Bay.
✉ Off the N59, 1.5km (1 mile) west of Recess ☎ 095-31001; www.cashel-house-hotel.com 🕒 Closed early Jan–early Feb

## CASTLEREA, CO ROSCOMMON
### Clonalis House (€€)
Clonalis House in Co Roscommon is the home of the O'Conors of Connacht, descendants of the Kings of Connacht and the last High King of Ireland. Guests here can browse through old family manuscripts and see the harp which belonged to the great Turlough O'Carolan.
✉ On the west side of Castlerea on the N60 ☎ 949-620014 🕒 Closed Oct to mid-Apr

## DOOLIN, CO CLARE
### Aran View House (€–€€)
This comfortable hotel is set in farmland, with views of the Aran Islands.
✉ Coast Road C065-7074061; www.aranview.com 🕒 Closed end Oct–Easter

## ENNISTYMON, CO CLARE
### Grovemount House (€)
A purpose-built guesthouse on the edge of the town, convenient for both The Burren and the Clare coast.
✉ Lahinch Road ☎ 065-7071431 🕒 Closed Nov–May

## GALWAY, CO GALWAY
### Glenlo Abbey (€€€)
Occupying an 18th-century abbey and in a landscaped estate overlooking a lough.

✉ Bushypark ☎ 091-526666; www.glenlo.com

### White House (€)
A guesthouse overlooking Galway Bay and The Burren, the White House has large, well-equipped bedrooms.

✉ 2 Ocean Wave, Salthill ☎ 091 529399; www.oceanbb.com

## ROUNDSTONE, CO GALWAY
### Eldon's (€–€€)
A distinctive blue-and-yellow painted building in this picturesque fishing village. Eldon's restaurant specializes in local seafood.

✉ Main Street ☎ 095-35933; www.eldons.ie ⏲ Closed Jan

# RESTAURANTS

## BALLYVAUGHAN, CO CLARE
### Hyland's Burren Hotel (€–€€)
Located close to the harbour, the hotel offers an excellent range of dishes. There is a popular bar menu for lunches.

✉ Ballyvaughan ☎ 065-7077037;www.hylandsburren.com ⏲ Lunch, dinner; closed Jan–Feb

### Monks Bar & Restaurant (€)
Renowned for its seafood chowder, Monks is a seafood speciality restaurant overlooking Galway Bay.

☎ 065-7077059 ⏲ Lunch, dinner

## CLARENBRIDGE, CO GALWAY
### Paddy Burke's (€–€€)
Famous as the focal point of the Clarenbridge Oyster Festival; no prizes for guessing the speciality dish.

☎ 091-796226; www.paddyburkesgalway.com ⏲ Lunch, dinner; closed Good Fri and 25 Dec

## CLIFDEN, CO GALWAY
### Mitchell's (€€)
Hearty Irish stew is the speciality here, with good portions of seafood and steaks from a varied menu.

✉ Market Street ☎ 095-21867 🕓 Lunch, dinner; closed mid-Nov to mid-Mar

## FOXFORD, CO MAYO
### Lough Cullin Room Restaurant (€€)
Fish and game dishes feature on the menu in this charming restaurant overlooking Lough Cullin.

✉ Healy's Hotel, Pontoon ☎ 094-925443 🕓 Dinner only

## GALWAY, CO GALWAY
### Kirbys of Cross Street (€–€€)
Good value contemporary cuisine on Irish themes, seasoned with influences from further afield.

✉ Cross Street ☎ 091-569404; www.kirbysrestaurant.com 🕓 Lunch, dinner

### Kirwan's Lane Restaurant (€€–€€€)
Stylish modern restaurant serving bistro-style grills and Asian influenced dishes..

✉ Kirwan's Lane ☎ 091-568266 🕓 Mon–Sat lunch and dinner, Sun dinner only; closed 25 Dec

### Trattoria Pasta Mista (€–€€)
You'll find fresh homemade pasta and traditional Italian dishes at this lively trattoria in the heart of the city.

✉ 12 Quay Street ☎ 091-563910 🕓 Dinner; call to check lunch times

### Tulsi Restaurant (€)
The Tulsi restaurant serves spicy tandoori specialities and biryani dishes, as well as seafood dishes and vegetarian options.

✉ Buttermilk Walk, Middle Street ☎ 091-569518 🕓 Lunch, dinner

## KILCOLGAN, CO GALWAY
### Morans Oyster Cottage (€–€€€)
Famous for its seafood. Specialities include chowder and smoked salmon.

✉ The Weir ☎ 091-796113; www.moransoystercottage.com ⏰ Lunch, dinner

## LISDOONVARNA, CO CLARE
### Sheedy's Country House Hotel (€€–€€€)
Set in lovely gardens, this family-run hotel-restaurant has an excellent reputation for its food and hospitality.

✉ Sheedy's Spa View Hotel ☎ 065-7074026 ⏰ Lunch (bar meals), dinner; closed mid-Oct to Easter

## MOYCULLEN, CO GALWAY
### White Gables Restaurant (€€–€€€)
This charming restaurant has an excellent reputation for its French cuisine and seafood.

☎ 091-555744; www.whitegables.com ⏰ Dinner Mon–Sat, lunch Sun only; closed 23 Dec to mid-Feb

## OILEÁIN ÁRANN (ARAN ISLANDS), CO GALWAY
### Mainistir House (€€)
Come here for a quirky dining experience overlooking the bay. The daily changing set menu is sure to please.

✉ Inis Mór (Inishmore) ☎ 099 61169; www.mainistirhouse.com ⏰ Daily: dinner at 8pm (one sitting only)

## RECESS, CO GALWAY
### Ballynahinch Castle (€€–€€€)
Local game, fish and fresh produce inspire the menus.

✉ On Roundstone road, off N59, 5km (3 miles) west of Recess ☎ 095-31006 ⏰ Lunch (bar meals), dinner; closed 29 Jan–23 Feb and 15–27 Dec

## ROUNDSTONE, CO GALWAY
### O'Dowd's Seafood Restaurant (€€)
Traditional pub with restaurant serving excellent Irish cooking
prepared using fresh locally caught fish.
✉ Roundstone ☎ 095-35809; www.odowdsrestaurant.com ⏰ Lunch, dinner

## SLIGO, CO SLIGO
### Embassy Rooms and The Belfry (€–€€)
Renowned for both its à la carte and its bar food.
✉ John F Kennedy Parade ☎ 071-9161250 ⏰ Lunch, dinner; closed Good
Fri, 25 Dec

### Fiddlers Creek (€€–€€€)
Good, wholesome steak and fish dishes served with an interesting
slant. Some tables overlook the river.
✉ Rockwood Parade ☎ 071-9141866 ⏰ Dinner daily; lunch Sun only

## WESTPORT, CO MAYO
### Asgard Bar and Restaurant (€€–€€€)
Overlooking Clew Bay; good seafood and Irish specialities.
✉ The Quay ☎ 098-25319 ⏰ Lunch, dinner; closed Mon and Tue off season

# SHOPPING

## CRAFTS
### Ballycasey Craft & Design Centre
Craftspeople here include: potters, goldsmith, florist and more.
✉ Shannon, Co Clare ☎ 061-364115

### Burren Perfumery
Demonstrations, displays, photographic exhibition and tea rooms.
✉ Carron, Co Clare ☎ 065-7089102 ⏰ Daily 9–5 (Jun–Sep to 7);
sometimes closed Jan

### Doolin Crafts Gallery
Crafts gallery run by batik artist and jewellery designer. Also sells
weaving and Irish instruments. Restaurant serving local produce.
✉ Doolin, Co Clare ☎ 065-7074309 ⏰ Daily (restaurant Apr–Oct)

### Foxford Woollen Mills Visitor Centre
Take a tour of the historic woollen mill. Also houses jewellery and woodcraft workshops and art gallery.
✉ Foxford, Co Mayo ☎ 094-9256104

### IDA Centre
Music, fashion and craft shops including pottery and jewellery. *Bodhrán*-making demonstrations. Café.
✉ Roundstone, Co Galway ☎ 095-35875

### Tús Craft Design Shop
This craft co-op centre displays ceramics, stained glass, painted silks, jewellery and delightful fairy dolls.
✉ Bridge Mills, Bridge Street, Galway, Co Galway ☎ 091-532500
🕐 Mon–Sat 10–6

## DEPARTMENT STORES
### Anthony Ryan's
All the usual departments, but specializes in women's wear.
✉ 6–18 Shop Street, Galway, Co Galway ☎ 091-567061

### Penneys
Fashions for everyone, good accessories department and household wares.
✉ Eyre Square Centre, Galway, Co Galway ☎ 091-566889/565095

## TRADITIONAL MUSIC
### Custy's Traditional Music Shop
Owned and staffed by experts.
✉ Francis Street, Ennis, Co Clare ☎ 065-6821727

### Mulligans
Stocks just about every traditional Irish music recording ever made, also jazz, blues, soul and country music.
✉ 5 Middle Street, Galway, Co Galway ☎ 091-564961

## ENTERTAINMENT

### LIVE MUSIC

**Bar Cuba**

Latin American and jazz.

✉ Eyre Square, Galway, Co Galway ☎ 091-565991

**The Roisin Dubh**

Traditional Irish, rock and pop in pub and on stage.

✉ 8 Upper Dominick Street, Galway, Co Galway ☎ 091-586540 ⏰ Nightly

**Tigh Colí**

Traditional music venue.

✉ Mainguard Street, Galway, Co Galway ☎ 091-561294 ⏰ Nightly at 6 and 9.30pm

### NIGHTCLUBS

**Boo Radley's Nightclub**

Clubbers can dance to music of top DJs on three floors.

✉ Eyre Square Hotel, Forster Street, Galway, Co Galway ☎ 091-569633

**Warwick**

Live bands and DJs draw in the crowds at this Salthill venue.

✉ O'Connor's Warwick Hotel, Salthill, Co Galway ☎ 091-521244 ⏰ Fri, Sat from 11pm

### THEATRES AND CINEMAS

**Claddagh Hall**

Traditional music and dance and folk drama.

✉ Nimmos Pier, Galway, Co Galway ☎ 091-755479/588044/755888
⏰ Mid-Jun to early Sep 8.45pm

**Galway Omniplex**

Premier cinema complex with the latest technology in projection and sound.

✉ Headford Road, Galway, Co Galway ☎ 091-567800

# The North

**When Brendan Behan said 'there is no such thing as bad publicity' he could not have contemplated the task of promoting the six counties of Northern Ireland (sometimes referred to as Ulster) as a tourist destination.**

The Province's unfortunate reputation deters many, and this is a great shame because they are missing some of the most beautiful scenery in Europe. The coast of Antrim offers a spectacular drive past the lovely Glens before swinging to the west to the Giant's

Causeway.

Further south the Mountains of Mourne sweep down to the sea. Inland are forest parks, lakes and mountains, historic towns, ancient sites and, of course, Belfast, a busy city with an industrial heritage and a lively arts scene. This section also includes the far northwestern part of the Republic, Co Donegal, famous for its beaches and tweed.

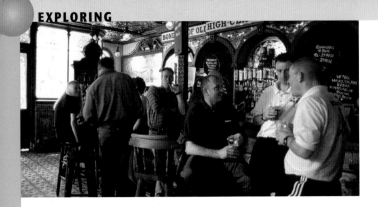

# Belfast

The capital of Northern Ireland is a relatively young city that grew rapidly in Victorian times, when its linen and shipbuilding industries flourished and the city doubled in size every 10 years. Today it has a unique character, brought about by the combination of hard work, hard times and a particular brand of Irish humour. The redevelopment of its dockyard areas continues to breathe new life and prosperity into the eastern flank of the city centre.

Belfast's industrial past, together with the disturbing images of the recent troubles, can conjure up a somewhat misleading picture for those who have never visited the city. Its Victorian prosperity has left a legacy of magnificent public buildings and monuments, finance houses and warehouses. At the heart of the city is the spacious and leafy Donegall Square, dominated by the magnificent City Hall, and the whole area is undergoing a huge makeover.

Belfast has superb museums, libraries and art galleries, excellent shopping and a lively and varied cultural life, from grand opera to informal traditional music sessions.

Beautiful parks and gardens include the famous Botanic Gardens and the canalside Lagan Valley Regional Park, but the most spectacular is on the slopes of Cave Hill to the north, which incorporates the zoo, Belfast Castle and a heritage centre.

🔀 10D

ℹ️ 59 North Street (☎ 028 9023 1221)

## BOTANIC GARDEN

The Botanic Garden is a wonderful place to wander away from the bustle of the city. It includes a fragrant rose garden, formal beds and herbaceous borders, and among the outstanding greenhouses is the Palm House. Begun in 1839, it is a remarkable cast-iron curvilinear structure in which tropical flowering plants thrive. Also in these lovely surroundings, the **Ulster Museum** gives a fascinating insight into the life and history of the Province. 'Made in Belfast' underlines the industry and inventiveness of Ulster (Northern Ireland) people, and there are many displays including 'Early Ireland' (10,000BC–1500BC).

➕ *Belfast 1a (off map)* ✉ Stranmills Road ☎ 028 9032 4902 🕐 Daily. Palm House: Apr–Sep Mon–Fri 10–5, Sat–Sun 2–5; Oct–Mar Mon–Fri 10–4, Sat–Sun 2–4. Closes for lunch ✋ Free 🚌 84, 85 🚉 Botanic Station

### Ulster Museum

☎ 028 9038 3000; www.ulstermuseum.org.uk 🕐 Mon–Fri 10–5, Sat 1–5, Sun 2–5 ✋ Free

## CITY HALL

In 1906 Belfast's City Hall was completed to mark the granting of city status by Queen Victoria. Set around a central courtyard, the building, of Portland stone, is topped by a tall copper dome which rises above the central staircase at the heart of an exuberant interior of rich mosaic, stained glass, marble and wood panelling.

✚ Belfast 2c ✉ Donegall Square ☎ 028 9027 0456 ⏰ Tours: Jun–Sep Mon–Fri 11, 2, 3, Sat 2.30; Oct–May Mon–Fri 11, 2.30, Sat 2.30 ✋ Free

## CROWN LIQUOR SALOON

High Victorian décor is preserved in this pub, in the care of the National Trust. It's a working pub managed by a brewery. The tiled exterior, with Corinthian pillars flanking the doorway, gives way to marble counters, stained glass, gleaming brass and ornately carved 'snugs'.

✚ Belfast 1b ✉ Great Victoria Street ☎ 028 9027 9901 ⏰ Mon–Sat 11.30–11, Sun 12.30–10 ✋ Free

## LAGAN LOOKOUT

Urban regeneration continues to progress in the 3-mile stretch of riverside known as Laganside. The £14 million Lagan Weir enabled a big clean-up of the river and Lagan Lookout tells the story of the project, including the history of the area and future plans. Visitors can see the weir, view the *Titanic* display, use interactive terminals and take a close-up look at one of the city's newest icons – the 10m (328ft) ceramic salmon, *The Big Fish*, by local sculptor, John Kindness.

✚ *Belfast 3d* ✉ Donegall Quay ☎ 028 9031 5444 🕐 Apr–Sep Mon–Fri 11–5, Sat noon–5, Sun 2–5; Oct–Mar Tue–Fri 11–3.30, Sat 1–4.30, Sun 2–4.30 ✋ Inexpensive

## ODYSSEY

Belfast's big millennium project was the building of this complex covering 9ha (23 acres) of the riverfront. It includes an interactive science centre with a special area for the under eights, an IMAX theatre, a 12-screen multiplex cinema and a huge arena, and the Pavilion has restaurants, bars and shops.

✚ *Belfast 4e* ✉ 2 Queen's Quay ☎ 028 9045 1055 ✋ Varies by attraction

# a walk around Belfast

**This walk starts in the heart of the city, then heads south along 'The Golden Mile' to visit the lovely Botanic Garden and the Ulster Museum.**

Donegall Square is surrounded by splendid architecture. Take a look at some of the statues and monuments in the grounds of City Hall before going inside (guided tours can be arranged in advance).

*Leave by the exit on the opposite side. Outside the gates of City Hall turn left along Donegall Square South. At the corner cross into May Street, then turn right into Alfred Street. Continue to reach St Malachy's on the left.*

St Malachy's was built in 1844 in castellated Gothic style with dark red brick and slender octagonal turrets. Inside there is fine fan-vaulting and an organ by Telford.

*From St Malachy's enter Clarence Street, turn left into Bedford Street, then bear right into Dublin Road and continue to Shaftesbury Square. Continue along Bradbury Place and fork left into University Road. Beyond the university, turn left to enter the Botanic Garden, where the Ulster Museum can be found.*

The beautiful Botanic Garden features a great Palm House and Tropical Ravine. Near by is the excellent Ulster Museum.

*Retrace your steps to Shaftesbury Square, then fork left to go along Great Victoria Street, passing the Crown Liquor Saloon on the right.*

Try to time the walk so that this famous National Trust pub, with its sumptuous and ornate Victorian interior, will be open.

*Continue past the Europa Hotel and the splendid Opera House, then turn right into Howard Street and return to Donegall Square.*

**Distance** About 4km (2.5 miles)
**Time** 3–4 hours, including cathedral, garden and museum visits
**Start/end point** Donegall Square ✚ Belfast 2c 🚌 All city centre buses
**Lunch** Crown Liquor Saloon (££) ✉ Great Victoria Street

# What to See in the North

### ARMAGH

Armagh is a distinguished city with a heritage of national importance. Nearby Navan Fort was the ancient capital of the kings of Ulster, and in AD445 St Patrick built his first church, on the site now occupied by St Patrick's Cathedral. From here the Irish were converted to Christianity and Armagh remains the ecclesiastical capital of Ireland. There has been much rebuilding of this Church of Ireland cathedral, but its core is medieval. There is also a Roman Catholic cathedral of St Patrick, finished in 1904, with a lavish interior of murals depicting Irish saints. **St Patrick's Trian,** in English Street, has an exhibition on the saint, along with the Land of Lilliput featuring Gulliver's travels. St Patrick was born about AD390 in Britain, the son of a Romano-British official. At 16 he was kidnapped by pirates and sold into slavery in Ireland, but later escaped due, he claimed, to divine intervention. This prompted his training for the ministry in Britain, before returnng to Ireland and establishing the Christian faith here.

The city has many other beautiful buildings in the old streets, and the stables of the former Archbishop's Palace have been converted into the excellent **Palace Stables Heritage Centre.**

✚ 9C 🚌 From Portadown Station 🚉 Portadown

**St Patrick's Trian**

www.saintpatrickstrian.com

✉ 40 English Street ☎ 028 3752 1801 🕐 Mon–Sat 10–5, Sun 2–5
🖐 Moderate 🍴 Restaurant (£)

**Palace Stables Heritage Centre**

⊠ Friary Road ☎ 028 3752 9629 🕔 Apr–Sep Sat–Sun 10–5 ✋ Moderate

🍴 Coffee shop (£), restaurant (£)

## BALLYCASTLE

Ballycastle, Co Antrim's largest town, is a popular seaside resort surrounded by some of Ireland's loveliest scenery. Nearby is the Carrick-a-Rede Rope Bridge, suspended 24.5m (80ft) above the sea, linking the clifftop to a rocky island, and from the harbour there are trips to Rathlin Island, one of the best places for birdwatching in Ireland.

On the edge of the town are the ruins of **Bonamargy Friary,** founded around 1500 and the burial place of the MacDonnell chiefs. At the end of August each year, the Diamond, at the centre of the town, is crammed with stalls, entertainments and horse-dealing of the famous Oul' Lammas Fair. **Ballycastle Museum** is housed in the 18th-century courthouse, and there is a Seafront Exhibition Centre with crafts and information.

➕ 10F 🚌 From Ballymoney Station

🚊 Ballymoney

**Bonamargy Friary**

⊠ Ballycastle

🕔 All year ✋ Free

**Ballycastle Museum**

⊠ 59 Castle Street

☎ 028 2076 2942

🕔 Jul–Aug (or by arrangement) Mon–Sat 12–6

✋ Free

## CARRICKFERGUS

Carrickfergus has the country's finest Norman **castle,** constructed on the edge of the sea in the late 12th century and still in use (as a magazine and armoury) as recently as 1928. Its impressive walls now house three floors of exhibitions and a medieval fair is held here each July.

There are remains of the 17th-century town walls, the earliest and largest urban defence in Ulster, including the North Gate, which has been rebuilt and restored.

Carrickfergus was the first footfall in Ireland of William of Orange, who landed here in 1690 for his victorious campaign against James II. Billy's Rock reputedly marks the exact spot.

Visit the unusual **Flame! The Gasworks Museum of Ireland,** Ireland's sole surviving coal gasworks, that supplied the town with gas for over 100 years until 1967.

➕ 10D 🚊 Carrickfergus

**Carrickfergus Castle**

✉ Marine Highway ☎ 028 9335 1273 🕐 Jun–Aug Mon–Sat 10–6, Sun 12–6; Apr, May, Sep Mon–Sat 10–6, Sun 2–6; Oct–Mar Mon–Sat 10–4, Sun 2–4 ✋ Moderate

**Flame! The Glassworks Museum of Ireland**

✉ 44 Irish Quarter West ☎ 028 9336 9575 🕐 Apr–Jun, Sep daily 2–6, Jul–Aug daily 10–6; Mar, Oct Sat–Sun 2–6 ✋ Inexpensive

## DONEGAL

Donegal Tweed has made the name of this northwest corner of Ireland familiar all around the world. It is a modest little town, but it has the remains of two castles and two abbeys, and is attractively set at the head of Donegal Bay. **Donegal Castle,** on the banks of the River Eske in the town centre, was built in 1505 for Red Hugh

O'Donnell and was considerably enlarged in the 17th century for Sir Basil Brooke. The Brooke family also owned Lough Eske Castle, a Jacobean-style house damaged by fire in 1939.

South of the town is **Donegal Abbey**. *The Annals of the Four Masters* was written here in the 17th century, charting the history of Ireland up until 1616. This important chronicle is now in the National Library in Dublin.

✚ 6D

### Donegal Castle
✉ Tinchonaill Street ☎ 074-9722405 ⏱ Mid-Mar to Nov, daily 10–6 (last admission 45 mins before closing) 🎫 Moderate

### Donegal Abbey
✉ Donegal ☎ Call Donegal tourist office: 074-9721148 ⏱ Daily
🍴 Refreshments (£)

## ENNISKILLEN

Enniskillen is attractively set on the River Erne between Upper and Lower Lough Erne. **Enniskillen Castle,** built in early 15th century, was the medieval stronghold of the Maguires and has a picturesque water gate. The keep now houses the Fermanagh Museum and a military museum. St Macartan's Cathedral is a small but interesting building, dating from the early 17th century, with some fine monuments and stained glass.

The Fermanagh Lakelands surrounding Enniskillen provide for all kinds of water-based leisure pursuits, and on Devenish Island is an important monastic site, founded in the 6th century by St Molaise. A little further afield is **Castle Coole,** designed by James Wyatt in 1795. The interiors are exquisite and the parkland runs down to the shores of Lough Coole. **Florence Court** is to the southwest, an 18th-century mansion noted for its rococo plasterwork.

✚ 7C

⛴ Ferry from Lower Lough Erne, 5km north of Enniskillen, to Devenish Island

**Enniskillen Castle**

✉ Castle Barracks, Wellington Road ☎ 028 6632 5000 🕐 Mon 2–5, Tue–Fri 10–5. Also open May–Sep Sat 2–5 (also Sun 2–5 Jul–Aug) ✋ Inexpensive
🚌 Ulster Bus Station

**Castle Coole**

☎ 028 6632 2690 🕐 Grounds: May–Sep daily 10–8; Oct–Apr daily 10–4. House: Mar to mid-May, Sep Sat–Sun 12–6; Jun–Aug daily 12–6 (closed Tue in Jun). Last tour 5.15 ✋ Moderate 🍴 Refreshments (£) 🚌 Ulsterbus 261 from Belfast to Enniskillen

**Florence Court**

✉ 12km (7.5 miles) southwest of Enniskillen ☎ 028 6634 8249/8497
🕐 Grounds: May–Sep daily 10–8; Oct–Apr daily 10–4. House: Jun–Aug daily; rest of year Sat–Sun and public hols 12–6 (last tour 5.15) ✋ Moderate
🍴 Tea room (£) 🚌 Ulsterbus 192 Enniskillen–Swanlinbar

## THE GIANT'S CAUSEWAY

See pages 42–43.

## THE GIANT'S CAUSEWAY COAST

The Giant's Causeway coast encompasses dramatic cliffs, wide sandy beaches, pretty fishing villages and clifftop castles. Portrush, the nearest large town, is a traditional seaside resort with two splendid beaches, and nearby is **Dunluce Castle,** a fairytale ruin which seems to grow out of the rock on which it is perched. Portballintrae is a pretty fishing village, made famous by the discovery in 1967 of the most valuable sunken treasure ever found on an Armada wreck – the *Girona* – which foundered here in 1588, with only five survivors from its crew of 1,300. The rescued treasure is now on display and can be seen in Belfast's Ulster Museum (➤ 161).

✚ 9–10F

**Dunluce Castle**

✉ 87 Dunluce Road, Bushmills ☎ 028 2073 1938 ✪ Jun–Aug Mon–Sat 10–6, Sun 12–6; Apr, May, Sep Mon–Sat 10–5, Sun 2–6; Oct–Mar Mon–Sat 10–4, Sun 2–4 ♿ Inexpensive 🚌 172 Portrush–Ballycastle

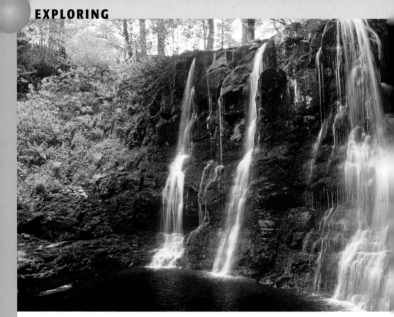

## THE GLENS OF ANTRIM

There are nine Glens of Antrim, lying roughly east of an imaginary line drawn between Ballycastle and Ballymena, and all of them are beautiful. There are wide valleys with a patchwork of green pastures, densely wooded mountain slopes and rocky gorges with tumbling streams dappled by the sunlight shining through the overhanging trees. Many of the glens are designated nature reserves and there are splendid walks, rich in wildlife and botanical interest and often with views to the coast. Millions of years of geological upheaval have formed these delightful valleys, which lie between the great plateau of the Antrim Mountains and a coastline that is justifiably described as the most scenic in the British Isles (▶ 174–175). Glenariff, the best known, has been dubbed the 'queen of the glens', and there is a wonderful view from the visitor centre.

✚ 10E

ℹ Tourist Information Centre: Sheskburn House, 7 Mary Street, Ballycastle

☎ 028 2076 2024

## LETTERKENNY

Letterkenny's long main street is overlooked by the Cathedral of St Eunan, built around 100 years ago and containing some important stained glass. The Donegal County Museum has artefacts from the Stone Age to medieval periods as well as more recent history and folk life. In Church Hill, on the shore of Lough Gartan, the lovely **Glebe House** is an art gallery, and just outside the town on the Glenties road is the Newmills Corn and Flax Mills.

✚ 7E

**Glebe House and Gallery**

✉ Churchill ☎ 074-9137071 ⏱ Easter and mid-May to late Sep 11–6.30. Closed Fri ✋ Inexpensive 🍴 Tea room (£)

## LONDONDERRY

Londonderry is a city that is historically absorbing, yet lively and

modern too. Take a guided walk of about 1.5km (1 mile) around its 17th-century town walls, which are still unbroken in spite of a 105-day siege by Jacobite forces in 1689, one of the most significant battles in Irish history. The city had hardly ever been trouble-free. Ever since St Columba founded his first monastery here in AD 546, its accessible location on the Foyle estuary attracted marauders. You can learn more of the history of the town at the **Tower Museum.**

Londonderry has impressive public buildings, two fine cathedrals and dramatic townscapes, but there are also lots of little lanes to explore, and behind the 19th-century Guildhall is the quay from which so many emigrants sailed for the New World.

✚ 8E

**Tower Museum**

✉ Union Hall Place ☎ 028 7137 2411 ⏱ Jul–Aug daily 10–4.30; Mar–Jan Mon–Sat 10–4.30; rest of year Mon–Fri 10–4.30 ✋ Moderate

🚉 Londonderry

# a drive around the Antrim coast

*From Larne take the A2 north signed Glenarm and the Antrim Coast Road.*

All the way to Ballycastle there is wonderful coastal scenery and pretty villages. Turn off to explore the Glens of Antrim if you have time.

*Pass Bonamargy Friary on the left and at the T-junction turn left into Ballycastle. From the Diamond take the A2 signposted 'Portrush, Bushmills, Giant's Causeway'. Soon turn right, signposted 'Ballintoy, B15, Coastal Route'. At the T-junction turn right and continue, passing the turning to Carrick-a-Rede Rope Bridge.*

In summer the rope bridge is strung high above the water across the gap between the mainland and a little rocky island.

*Go through Ballintoy and after 5.5km (3.5 miles) turn right into Causeway Road. After another 5.5km (3.5 miles) you reach the Visitor Centre.*

This is a World Heritage Site and a unique phenomenon which should not be missed.

*From the Causeway, take the A2 to Bushmills and at the roundabout in the village go straight on, signposted 'Dervock'. After a short distance, reach the Bushmills Distillery on the left.*

Though it is a large-scale working distillery, Bushmills is well prepared for visitors, with an interesting and entertaining tour, tastings and shops.

*Continue to Dervock, then at T-junction turn right with the B66, signposted 'Ballymoney'. About 6.5km (4 miles) farther on turn left on to the A26. Stay on this road and at the end of its short motorway section, reach a roundabout and turn left onto A36. From here follow signs back to Larne.*

**Distance** 160km (100 miles)
**Time** About 7 hours
**Start/end point** Larne ✚ 10E
**Lunch** Wysner's (£) ✉ 16 Ann Street, Ballycastle ☎ 028 2076 2372

## LOUGH NEAGH

Lough Neagh, the largest lake in the British Isles, has little hidden harbours, sandy beaches and a number of islands. Lakes are always best explored by boat, and Lough Neagh is no exception, because the roads around it rarely follow the waterline. The *Irish Mist* cruises around the lake from the marina at Antrim, a busy and attractive town, with a famous 9th-century round tower.

In the southeastern corner of the lough, Oxford Island has a range of habitats for birdlife, including wet meadows, reedbeds, woodlands and shoreline scrub. The **Lough Neagh Discovery Centre** here has audio-visual shows and interactive games, and visitors can participate in guided walks or take a boat trip.

For more seclusion, there are hides (camouflaged shelters) for birdwatching and a variety of marked walking trails.

✚ 9D

**Lough Neagh Discovery Centre**

✉ Oxford Island ☎ 028 3832 2205 🕓 Apr–Sep daily 10–6 (until 7 Sun); Oct, Mar Mon–Sun 10–5 ✋ Moderate 🍽 Cafe (££)

## MOUNTAINS OF MOURNE

Percy French wrote many popular songs extolling the beauty of Ireland, but his best-known line must surely be *'where the Mountains of Mourne sweep down to the sea'*. Few first-time visitors, though, would be prepared for the wild beauty of the scenery.

The **Mourne Heritage Trust** at Newcastle is a good place to start, with lots of information and guided walks. One of the nature trails follows the 'Brandy Pad', a notorious smugglers' route that links Hilltown, appropriately notable for its many pubs, with the coast south of Newcastle.

Slieve Donard, at 839m (2,752ft), is the highest mountain, and clothing its slopes is the Donard Forest Park. There is more woodland in the Tollymore and Castlewellan forest parks, while to the south is the evocatively named Silent Valley, flooded to form two great reservoirs. There is a charge for cars to enter the forest parks and Silent Valley, which are accessible from about 10am (closing time varies depending on the season).

✚ 10C

**Mourne Heritage Trust**

**www.**mournealive.com

✉ 87 Central Promenade, Newcastle ☎ 028 4372 4059 ⏰ Mon–Fri 9–5

✋ Free

## MOUNT STEWART HOUSE AND GARDENS

One of Ireland's grandest stately homes, Mount Stewart was built for the 3rd Marquess of Londonderry. Three architects were involved in the building – James Wyatt, in the 1780s, then George Dance and (probably) William Vitruvious Morrison in the early 19th century. The imposing interior largely reflects the impeccable taste of the 7th Marchioness, a leader of London society in the 1920s and 1930s. She was also responsible for the garden, which benefits from the mild climate between the Irish Sea and Strangford Lough.

➕ 11D ✉ 8km (5 miles) southeast of Newtownards ☎ 028 4278 8387
🕐 Grounds: May–Sep daily 10–8; Apr,Oct daily 10–6; Nov–Mar daily 10–4.
House: Jul–Aug daily 12–6; May–Jun, Sep Mon, Wed-Fri 1–6, Sat–Sun 12–6;
mid-Mar to Apr, Oct Sat–Sun and public hols 12–6 ✋ Moderate 🍴 Tea room
(£) 🚌 Ulsterbus 9 and 10 from Belfast–Portaferry 🚉 Bangor

## ULSTER-AMERICAN FOLK PARK

See pages 54–55.

## ULSTER FOLK AND TRANSPORT MUSEUM

All kinds of Ulster buildings have been painstakingly dismantled in their original locations, brought to this 25ha (72-acre) site and reconstructed in appropriate settings, including a small town of the 1900s, complete with shops, a school, churches, printer's workshops, a bank and terraced houses. Rural exhibits include traditional Irish cottages, watermills and farmhouses, and farming is represented by rare breeds of animals and fields which are cultivated using traditional methods.

The Transport Museum is comprehensive, covering all forms of transport from horse-drawn carts to the De Lorean car, and includes the superb Irish Railway Collection and The Flight Experience, an interactive exhibition. Perennially popular is the *Titanic* exhibition, about the 'unsinkable' liner which was built in Belfast's shipyards and foundered after hitting an iceberg on her maiden voyage.

As well as the permanent exhibitions, the museum has special events, which change from year to year.

**www.uftm.org.uk**

➕ 10D ✉ Bangor Road, Cultra, Holywood ☎ 028 9042 8428 🕓 Mar–Jun Mon–Sat 10–6, Sun 11–6; Jul–Sep Mon–Sat 10–6, Sun 11–6; Oct–Feb Mon–Fri 10–4, Sat 10–5, Sun 11–5 🖑 Moderate 🍴 Tea room (£) 🚌 B1, B2 from Belfast to Bangor 🚉 Cultra Halt

## WELLBROOK BEETLING MILL

This water-powered 18th-century linen hammer mill, set in a lovely wooded glen on the banks of the fast-flowing River Ballinderry, is a testament to the history of linen-making in Northern Ireland. For much of the 19th century the north of Ireland was the world's greatest producer of linen and you can see demonstrations of how the material was made. Tours are conducted around the mill, costumed interpreters explain the process of manufacture and you can try your hand at scutching, hackling, weaving and beetling. Beetling is the final process in linen manufacture, when the cloth is repeatedly hammered to prodce a sheen – the heavy wooden hammers used were known as beetles. The process could last for anything between two days and two weeks. The mill's seven water-powered beetling engines create a thunderous noise and it is said that it was not unusual for the beetlers to become completely or partially deaf working in a confined space for up to 15 hours a day.

➕ 9D ✉ Wellbrook Road, Corkhill (6.5km/4 miles west of Cookstown) ☎ 028 8674 8210 🕓 Mid-Mar to Jun and Sep Sat–Sun 11–6; Jul–Aug daily 11–6 🖑 Moderate 🚌 Ulsterbus 90 from Cookstown, request stop at Kildress then 1km (half-mile) walk ❓ Shop; scenic walks

# HOTELS

## ARMAGH, CO ARMAGH
### Hillview Lodge (££)
Family-run guesthouse with good facilities in a rural setting just a mile from the city. Golf driving range.

✉ 33 Newtownhamilton Road ☎ 028 3752 2000; www.hillviewlodge.com

## BALLINTOY, CO ANTRIM
### Whitepark House (££)
Country house on the coast road between the Causeway and the rope bridge.

✉ 150 Whitepark Road ☎ 028 2073 1482; www.whiteparkhouse.com

## BELFAST, CO ANTRIM
### Ash-Rowan Town House (££)
Former home of Thomas Andrews, designer of the *Titanic*. The quality furnishings are popular with guests here.

✉ 12 Windsor Avenue ☎ 028 9066 1758

### Hastings Europa Hotel (£££)
The Europa is a truly international hotel with excellent facilities and was the choice of President Clinton during his visit to Belfast. It was once famed for being 'the most bombed hotel' but can now be described as luxurious.

✉ Great Victoria Street ☎ 028 9027 1066; www.hastingshotel.com

### Jury's Belfast Inn (££)
In the heart of the city, next to the Opera House, a short walk from the main shopping area.

✉ Fisherwick Place, Great Victoria Street ☎ 028 9053 3500; www.jurysdoyle.com

### Malmaison Belfast (£££)
This luxury hotel has an Italianate façade and superbly styled bedrooms.

✉ 34–38 Victoria Street ☎ 028 9022 0200; www.malmaison.com

## CARNLOUGH, CO ANTRIM
### Londonderry Arms Hotel (££–£££)
Famous for its food and its history, this fine Georgian house was once owned by Sir Winston Churchill.

✉ 20 Harbour Road ☎ 028 2888 5255; www.glensofantrim.com

## COLERAINE, CO LONDONDERRY
### Breezemount House (££)
Restored 19th-century house offering superior bed-and-breakfast facilities. All rooms have private bathroom, own kitchen and satellite TV.

✉ 26 Castlerock Road ☎ 028 7034 4615; www.breezemount.co.uk
🕐 Closed 24–8 Dec

## DONEGAL, CO DONEGAL
### Central Hotel (££–£££)
Family-run town-centre hotel with views over Donegal Bay from the garden.

✉ The Diamond ☎ 074-9721027; www.whites-hotelsireland.com

### Harvey's Point (££)
On Lough Eske's shore, this modern hotel has spacious bedrooms and fine cuisine.

✉ Lough Eske, on N56 ☎ 074-9722208; www.harveyspoint.com 🕐 Closed Mon–Tue Nov–Mar

## ENNISKILLEN, CO FERMANAGH
### Arch House Tullyhona (£)
Comfortable, welcoming guesthouse, good for families with young children.

✉ 59 Marble Arch Road ☎ 028 6634 8452; www.archhouse.com

## LONDONDERRY, CO LONDONDERRY
### Trinity Hotel (£££)
Bright new city-centre hotel.

✉ 22–24 Strand Road ☎ 028 7127 1271

## RESTAURANTS

### ANNALONG, CO DOWN
**Glassdrumman Lodge (£££)**
Prime local produce, including prawns and salmon, feature on the six-course dinner menu of well-produced dishes.
✉ 85 Mill Road ☎ 028 4376 8451 ⏰ Dinner; bookings essential

### BALLYCASTLE, CO ANTRIM
**Wysner's (£–££)**
Pleasant two-storey restaurant in the centre of town, with reasonably priced dishes, including traditional Irish and a good selection of healthy eating options.
✉ 16 Ann Street ☎ 028 2076 2372 ⏰ Lunch, dinner; closed Sun

### BALLYMENA, CO ANTRIM
**Galgorm Resort and Spa (££–£££)**
The new restaurant of this restored 19th-century mansion offers fine dining overlooking the River Maine.
✉ 136 Fenaghy Road ☎ 028 2588 1001 ⏰ Lunch, dinner

### BANGOR, CO DOWN
**Clandeboye Lodge Hotel (£)**
Interesting treatment of good local produce in a secluded location.
✉ 10 Estate Road, Clandeboye ☎ 028 9185 2500 Lunch, dinner, bar food; closed 24–26 Dec

### BELFAST, CO ANTRIM
**Morning Star (££)**
An historic Belfast pub with exceptionally good food, using only the freshest Ulster produce and seafood.
✉ 17 Pottinger's Entry ☎ 028 9032 3976 ⏰ Lunch daily, dinner Mon–Sat

**Nick's Warehouse (££)**
See page 59.

**The Northern Wing (£–££)**
Caesar salad, beef and Guinness sausages, salmon goujons

(strips) and more served in this in this old printing press now restored into a stylish restaurant.

✉ 2 Bridge Street ☎ 028 9050 9888 🕐 All day menu

## Olio (£)

Warm and welcoming restaurant offering a range of European and Cajun dishes.

✉ 17 Brunswick Street ☎ 028 9024 0239 🕐 Noon–10pm (11 Fri, Sat); closed Sun

## Shu (££–£££)

Cosmopolitan brasserie-style restaurant, which has received many accolades since opening in 2000.

✉ 252 Lisburn Road ☎ 028 9038 1655; www.shu-restaurant.com 🕐 Lunch, dinner; closed Sun

## DONEGAL, CO DONEGAL
### Harbour Restaurant (£–££)

Cosy restaurant with a good variety of international and Irish dishes.

✉ Quay Street ☎ 074-9721702 🕐 Lunch Sun, dinner daily

## ENNISKILLEN, CO FERMANAGH
### Killyhevlin Hotel (£–££)

Excellent food and wonderful views over Lough Erne.

✉ Dublin Road, Killyhevlin ☎ 028 6632 3481 🕐 Breakfast, lunch, dinner

## HILLSBOROUGH, CO DOWN
### Hillside Restaurant and Bar (££)

Traditional country-house cooking with global influences.

✉ 21 Main Street ☎ 028 9268 2765 🕐 Bar: lunch, dinner. Restaurant: dinner Fri, Sat; closed evenings Good Fri and 25 Dec

## KILLYLEAGH, CO DOWN
### Dufferin Arms (£–££)

European, seafood and vegetarian choices feature heavily on the menu at this well-known country pub.

✉ 35 High Street ☎ 028 4482 1182 🕐 Lunch, dinner

## LIMAVADY, CO LONDONDERRY
### The Lime Tree (££)
Modern Irish cuisine using the best of seasonal local produce.
✉ 60 Catherine Street ☎ 028 7776 4300 🕓 Dinner only Tue–Sat; closed 25–26 Dec

## LONDONDERRY, CO LONDONDERRY
### Beech Hill Country House Hotel (££–£££)
This exclusive hotel in a peaceful location in 13ha (32 acres) of glorious woodlands has an excellent restaurant.
✉ 32 Ardmore Road ☎ 028 7134 9279; www.beech-hill.com 🕓 Breakfast, lunch, dinner; closed 25 Dec

## OMAGH, CO TYRONE
### Mellon Country Inn (££)
The Mellon serves up traditional Irish cuisine with a modern twist.
✉ 134 Beltany Road ☎ 028 8166 1224 🕓 Lunch, dinner

## PORTAFERRY, CO DOWN
### Portaferry Hotel (£££)
A charming 18th-century inn picturesquely set on the edge of Strangford Lough. The restaurant is best known for its seafood.
✉ 10 The Strand ☎ 028 4272 8231 🕓 Lunch, early evening menu, à la carte dinner; closed 24–5 Dec

# SHOPPING

## CRAFTS
### Bonners of Ardara
Bonners, world-renowned for the quality of their knitwear, have a factory in the town and employ more than 500 hand-knitters throughout Donegal. Also sells Waterford Crystal, Belleek and Donegal china, jewellery, linens and tweeds.
✉ Front Street, Ardara, Co Donegal ☎ 074-9541303 🕓 May–Jun Mon–Sat 9–6.30; Jul–Aug Mon–Sat 10–7, Sun 10–6; Sep–Apr Mon–Tue Thu–Sat 10–6

### Conway Mill Craft Shop

Over 22 artists work within this old mill and display their work in the craft shop, which sometimes hosts other events such as book or poetry readings. Items of contemporary and Irish art. Also guided tours of the mill.

✉ 5–7 Conway Street, Belfast, Co Antrim ☎ 028 9032 6452
🕐 Mon–Fri 10–4

### Donegal Craft Village

Variety of items, including pottery, Uilleann pipes, jewellery, batik and woven goods. Coffee shop.

✉ Ballyshannon Road, Donegal, Co Donegal ☎ 074- 9722225 🕐 Mon–Sat 10–5.30 (sometimes closed winter)

### Derry Craft Village

Craftspeople ply their trade in an 18th-century setting.

✉ Shipquay Street, Londonderry, Co Londonderry ☎ 028-7126 0329
🕐 Daily 9–6 or 7

### Tyrone Crystal

Guided tour takes in all the stages of producing fine crystal, from glass-blowing to cutting and finishing.

✉ Killybrackey, Coalisland Road, Dungannon, Co Tyrone ☎ 028 8772 5335
🕐 Shop: Mon–Sat 9.30–5, Sun 1–5 (seasonal). Tours: Mon–Fri 11, 12, 2, 3

### The Wicker Man

Highly regarded craft shop showcasing work by over 150 Irish craftspeople.

✉ 14 Donegal Arcade, Castle Place, Belfast, Co Antrim ☎ 028 9024 3550
🕐 Mon–Sat 9–5.30 (to 9pm Thu)

## DEPARTMENT STORE

### Magee's

A legend in the world of department stores, run by the same family since 1866. The speciality is hand-woven Donegal tweed; guided tours of original looms at work.

✉ The Diamond, Donegal, Co Donegal ☎ 074-9722660

## MARKET
### St George's Market
Built in 1896, the market has had a face-lift.

✉ Oxford Street/May Street, Belfast, Co Antrim ⏰ Fri morning and Sat 10–4

## TRADITIONAL MUSIC
### Premier Record Store
Specializes in traditional CDs and tapes. Behind Castle Court Shopping Centre.

✉ 3–5 Smithfield Square North, Belfast, Co Antrim ☎ 028 9024 0896

### Stillsounds
Every genre of music is catered for here, both new and second-hand.

✉ 22A Waterloo Street, Londonderry, Co Londonderry ☎ 028 7128 8890

# ENTERTAINMENT

## LIVE MUSIC
### Dungloe Bar
✉ Waterloo Street, Londonderry, Co Londonderry ☎ 028 7126 7716

### John Hewitt Bar
In the heart of the Cathedral quarter, this very traditional bar stages jazz on Friday and traditional music on Tuesday, Wednesday and Saturday.

✉ 51 Donegall Street, Belfast, Co Antrim ☎ 028 9023 3768

### Robinsons
Five bars, each with it's own style.

✉ 38–42 Great Victoria Street, Co Antrim ☎ 028 9024 7447

### Rotterdam Bar
Probably the most famous of Belfast's music pubs. Bands play outside in summer, attracting huge crowds into Barrow Square.

✉ 54 Pilot Street, Co Antrim ☎ 028 9074 6021

## NIGHTCLUBS
### Club Milk
Offers a varied spectrum of music, from house to disco.
✉ 10–14 Tomb Street, Belfast, Co Antrim ☎ 028 9027 8876 🕓 Nightly

### The Fly Bar
Sophisticated cocktails and Cool FM DJs.
✉ 5–6 Lower Crescent, Belfast, Co Antrim ☎ 028 9050 9750

### Front Page
Pub club with live bands.
✉ Lower Donegall Street, Belfast, Co Antrim ☎ 028 9032 4924

## THEATRE AND CINEMA
### The Movie House
✉ Yorkgate Shopping Complex, York Street, Belfast, Co Antrim ☎ 028 9075 5000

### Nerve Centre
Innovative, multimedia arts centre.
✉ Londonderry, Co Londonderry ☎ 028 7126 0562

### Old Museum Arts Centre
A venue for experimental theatre, dance, story-telling and poetry.
✉ College Square North, Belfast, Co Antrim ☎ 028 9023 3332

### Queen's Film Theatre
✉ University Square Mews, Belfast, Co Antrim ☎ 0800 9097 1097

### Verbal Arts Centre
Children's events, storytelling and more.
✉ London Street, Londonderry, Co Londonderry ☎ 028 7126 6946

# Index

accommodation 103–104, 129–130, 152–153, 180–181
activities 64–65
agriculture 11
Aillwee Cave 143
air travel 26, 28
angling 11, 64
Antrim 176
Antrim coast 174–175
Aqua Dome 71
Aran Islands *see* Oileáin Árann
Armada Exhibition 125
Armagh 166–167
Athlone 149

Ballycastle 167
banks 31
Bantry 118, 125
Bantry House 118, 125
Beara Peninsula 118–119
Belfast 160–165
Belfast Zoo 70
birdlife 64
Blarney Castle 119
Blasket Islands 40
boat trips 66–67
Bonamargy Friary 167
Botanic Garden, Belfast 161, 165
breakdowns 27
breath-testing 27
Brú Ború Heritage Centre 120–121
Brú na Bóinne 36–37
Bunratty Castle and Folk Park 142–143
the Burren 143
buses 28–29
Bushmills Distillery 175

Caherdaniel 122
Cahersiveen 122
car rental 29
Carrantuohill 11
Carrick-a-Rede Rope Bridge 167, 174–175
Carrick-on-Shannon 149
Carrickfergus 168
Cashel 120–121
Castle Coole 170
Castlebar 144
Castletown House 90–91
Castlewellan Forest Park 177
Cathedral of Our Lady Assumed into Heaven and St Nicholas 138–139, 141
Causeway School Museum 43

Causeway Visitor Centre 43
Ceanannus Mór (Kells) 91
*ceilidhs* 16–17
Chester Beatty Library 82
children's entertainment 70–71
Christ Church Cathedral 75
Cill Rónáin (Kilronan) 50
cinemas 110, 136, 158, 187
City Hall, Belfast 162, 164
The Claddagh 138
Clarenbridge 19
Cliffs of Moher 17, 144
climate 22, 32
Clonmacnoise 38–39
Clonmacnoise & West Offaly Railway 71
clothing sizes 33
concessions 29
Connemara 145
Connemara National Park 145
Coolatin Park 102
Corca Dhuibhne (Dingle Peninsula) 40–41
Cork 112–117
Cork Butter Museum 113, 117
Cork City Gaol 113
Cork Public Museum 114, 117
crafts 44, 108–109, 134, 156–157, 184–185
Crawford Art Gallery 114, 116
Crown Liquor Saloon, Belfast 162, 165
cruising 64
The Curragh 17
currency 32
cycling 64

DART (Dublin Area Rapid Transit) 28
dental services 23
Devenish Island 170
Dingle Oceanworld 70
Dingle Peninsula *see* Corca Dhuibhne
Donard Forest Park 177
Donegal 168–169
Donegal Abbey 169
Donegal Castle 168–169
Dowth 37
drinking water 33
drives
    Antrim coast 174–175
    Connemara 146–147
    Kerry and Cork 124–125
    Wicklow Mountains 100–101
driving 27
Dublin 17, 74–75, 82–89

Dublin Castle 75, 82
Dublin Writers Museum 83
Dublin Zoo 70
Dún Aonghasa 50
Dún Eochla 50
Dunluce Castle 171
Dvblinia 75, 84

eating out 58–59, 104–107, 130–133, 153–156, 182–184
electricity 31–32
embassies and consulates 30
emergency telephone numbers 30
Enniskillen 170
entertainment 109–110, 135–136, 158, 186–187
Erne, waterway 64

Fermanagh Lakelands 170
ferries 26–27, 29
festivals and events 24–25
fishing 11, 64
Florence Court 170
Folk Village 120, 121
food and drink 12–15, 19
    *see also* eating out
Fota Wildlife Park 71
fuel 27
Fungi the Dolphin 40, 66

Gaelic sports 64
Gallarus Oratory 40
Galway 138–141
Garinish Island 124
geography 11
Giant's Causeway 19, 42–43
Giant's Causeway Coast 171
Glebe House, Letterkenny 173
Glen of the Dargle 98
Glenariff 172
Glendalough 17, 92–93, 101
Glengarriff 118, 124
Glens of Antrim 172
golf 11, 64
Guinness 14–15, 60
Guinness Storehouse 84–85

health advice 22, 23, 32–33
Healy Pass 118, 124
Hell Fire Club 102
horse-back riding 65
horse racing 65
Hunt Museum 127

Inis Meáin (Inishmaan) 50
Inis Mór (Inishmore) 50

Inis Oírr (Inisheer) 50
insurance 22, 23
Irish Agricultural Museum 99
Irish Horse Museum 17
Irish National Heritage Park 93
Isle of Inisfree 150

Jameson Heritage Centre 69
Japanese Gardens 95
jaunting cars and jarveys 123
Jerpoint Abbey 94

Kells see Ceanannus Mór
Kenmare 121
Kildare 94–95
Kilkenny 44–45
Kilkenny Castle 44, 45
Kilkenny Design Centre 44, 45, 109
Killarney 122–123
Killarney National Park 123
Killorglin 122
Kilmainham Gaol 85
Kilmalkedar Church 40–41
Kilronan 50
King John's Castle 127
Kinsale 126
Knappogue Castle 148
Knowth 37
Kylemore Abbey 148–149

Lagan Lookout, Belfast 163
Leisureland 71
Letterkenny 173
Limerick 127
literary figures 76–77
local ways and attitudes 60
Londonderry 173
long distance buses 28
Lough Neagh 11, 176

Macgillicuddy's Reeks 11
Malahide 96–97
markets 134, 186
Minard Castle 40
Mitchelstown Caves 70
Monasterboice 97
money 32
Mount Stewart House and Gardens 178
Mount Usher Gardens 100
mountains 11, 100–101, 102, 177
Mourne Mountains 177
Muckross House 46–47, 124
Museum of Country Life 144

music, traditional 72–73, 109, 135, 157

National Gallery of Ireland 86
national holidays 25
National Museum, Dublin 48–49, 74
National Stud 95
National Wax Museum 87
Newgrange 36–37
Newmills Corn & Flax Mills 173
nightlife 110, 136, 158, 187
Nora Barnacle House Museum 139, 141

O'Brien's Tower 144
Odyssey, Belfast 163
Oileáin Árann (Aran Islands) 50–51
Old Jameson Distillery 87
opening hours 31

Parknasilla 122
passports and visas 22
personal safety 33
pharmacies 32
photography 33
police 33
Portballintrae 171
Portrush 171
postal services 31
Poulaphouca Reservoir 102
Powerscourt House and Gardens 98, 100, 102
public transport 28–29
pubs 135–136, 158, 186

racehorses 17, 95
Rathlin Island 167
Ring of Kerry 16, 122
Rothe House 44, 45
Rock of Cashel 52–53
Roundstone 146–147

St Anne's Church, Cork 114, 117
St Fiachra's Garden 95
St Nicholas's Church, Galway 139, 141
St Patrick 52–53, 166
sailing 65
Sally Gap 102
Salthill 138
seat belts 27
senior citizens 29
Shannon, River 11, 19, 64, 149

shopping 32, 68–69, 107–109, 133–135, 156–157, 184–186
Silent Valley 177
Skibbereen 17–18
Slieve Donard 177
Sligo 150
Spanish Arch 138, 140
speed limits 27
sport and leisure 11, 64–65
students 29
Sub-Tropical Gardens 118–119

taxis 29
telephones 30–31
Temple Bar 88
theatres 110, 136, 158, 187
Thoor Ballylee 151
time differences 23
tipping 32
Tollymore Forest Park 177
tourist offices 23, 30
trains 28
travelling to Ireland 26–27
Trinity College 74, 88–89

Ulster-American Folk Park 54–55
Ulster Folk and Transport Museum 178–179
Ulster Museum 161
urban buses 28–29

Ventry 40
views 62–63
Viking Splash Tour 71

W5 70
walks
around Belfast 164–165
around Cork 116–117
around Dublin 74–75
walking 65
Waterford 128
Waterford crystal 128
websites 23
Wellbrook Beetling Mill 179
Westport 150–151
Westport House 150–151
Wexford 98–99
Wexford Wildfowl Reserve 99
whiskey and beer 14–15
Wicklow Gap 102
Wicklow Mountains 100–101, 102

Yeats, W B 77, 151
Yeats Tower 151

# Acknowledgements

The Automobile Association would like to thank the following photographers and companies for their assistance in the preparation of this book.

Abbreviations for the picture credits are as follows – (t) top; (b) bottom; (c) centre; (l) left; (r) right; (AA) AA World Travel Library

**4l** Dunmanus Bay, Co Cork, AA/J Blandford; **4c** Ferries at Rosslare, AA/C Jones; **4r** St Candice Cathedral, Kilkenny, AA/M Short; **5l** Ha'Penny Bridge, Dublin, AA/S Whitehorne; **5c** Powerscourt Estate, AA/L Blake; **6/7** Dunmanus Bay, Co Cork, AA/J Blandford; **8/9** St Colman's Cathedral, Cobh, AA/D Forss; **10/11t** O'Connell Street, Dublin, AA/S Day; **10cl** Rock of Cashel, AA/S McBride; **10cr** Dingle, AA/C Jones; **11c** Bar, Dublin, AA/S Whitehorne; **11b** Pony trap, Muckross estate, AA/J Blandford; **12b** Powerscourt Shopping Centre, Dublin, AA/M Short; **13tr** English Market, Cork, AA/S Hill; **13c** Food market, Dublin, AA/S Day; **14l** St Patrick's Street, Cork, AA/C Jones; **14r** Old Jameson Distillery, Dublin, AA/S Day; **15t** Guinness, AA/C Coe; **15b** Dublin, AA/S Day; **16/17t** Grafton Street, Dublin, AA/S Day; **16/17c** The Curragh, AA/C Coe; **16b** Derrynane and the Ring of Kerry, AA/J Blandford; **17b** Cliffs of Moher, AA/P Zollier; **18** Giant's Causeway, AA/C Hill; **19t** Galway Oyster Festival, AA/S McBride; **19b** Athlone Castle, AA/L Blake; **20/21** Ferries at Rosslare, AA/C Jones; **24** Galway oyster festival, AA/S McBride; **26t** Airport terminal, Digitalvision; **26/27b** Lough Leane, Co Kerry, AA/J Blandford; **27t** Road between Glengarriff and Kenmare, AA; **28cl** Dart train, AA/M Short; **29** Road signs, AA/M Diggin; **30** City tour bus, AA/S Day; **31** Post box, AA/S Whitehorne; **33** Garda car, AA/J Dawson; **34/35** St Candice Cathedral, Kilkenny, AA/M Short; **36/37t** Inscribed stones, AA/M Short; **36/37b** Newgrange, AA/P Zollier; **37cl** Mace head, Knowth, AA/C Coe; **38bl** Nun's Church, AA/C Coe; **38/39** Clonmacnois, AA/L Blake; **39tr** Bay near Clonmacnois, AA/S McBride; **40t** Dingle, AA/C Jones; **40c** Stone cross, Kilmalkedar Church, AA/C Jones; **41** Slea head, Dingle peninsula, AA/C Jones; **42/43** Giant's Causeway, AA/C Coe; **44cl** Kilkenny, AA/S McBride; **44bl** Kilkenny, AA/S McBride; **45** Kilkenny Castle, AA/C Jones; **46** Muckross House, AA/J Blandford; **46/47b** Muckross House, K Welsh/Alamy; **48/49t** National Museum, AA/S Whitehorne; **48b** National Museum, AA/S Day; **50t** Celtic cross, Inishmore, AA/S Hill; **50c** Dun Aengus, Inishmore Island, AA/S Hill; **51** Collecting seaweed, AA/Stephen Hill; **52** Rock of Cashel, AA/S McBride; **53tl** Shamrock motif, Rock of Cashel, AA/S McBride; **53tr** Tomb, Rock of Cashel, AA/S McBride; **54/55t** 19th-century street of shops, Ulster-American Folk Park; **54c** Mellon farmhouse, Ulster-American Folk Park; **56/57t** Ha'Penny Bridge, Dublin, AA/S Whitehorne; **58** Restaurant, Dublin, AA/S McBride; **61** Stag's Head pub, Dublin, AA/S McBride; **62/63** Connemara National Park, AA/C Jones; **65** Golfers, Ballybunion, AA/P Zollier; **66/67** Lough Erne, Co Kerry, AA/C Coe; **68** Belleek Pottery workshop, AA/J Johnson; **70/71bg** Viking Splash Tour, AA/S Day; **73** Fitzsimon's Inn, Dublin, AA/S Day; **74** Christ Church Cathedral, AA/S Whitehorne; **75tl** Dublin Castle, AA/S Day; **75tr** Temple Bar, AA/S Day; **76** Monument to W B Yeats, Sligo Town, AA/C Hill; **77** Shaw Birthplace, Dublin, AA/S Day; **78/79** Powerscourt Estate, AA/L Blake; **81** South cross, Kells, AA/P Zollier; **83t** Record Tower, Dublin Castle, AA/S Day; **83b** Brendan Behan's typewriter, AA/S Day; **84** Atrium, Guinness Storehouse; **85t** Guinness Storehouse; **85b** Kilmainham Gaol AA/S Whitehorne; **86** National Gallery, AA/Slide File; **87** Old Jameson Distillery, AA/S Day; **88l** Trinity College, AA/L Blake; **88/89** Temple Bar, AA/S Day; **90/91** Castletown House, AA/M Short; **92t** Glendalough, AA/C Jones; **92cb** Glendalough, AA/C Jones; **93b** Irish National Heritage Park, AA/P Zollier; **94l** Jerpoint Abbey, AA/M Short; **95t** Japanese Gardens, AA/S McBride; **95c** Japanese Gardens, AA/M Short; **96/97** Malahide Castle, AA/Slide File; **97r** Cross of Muiredach, AA/C Jones; **98tr** Powerscourt Gardens, AA/M Short; **99** Wexford AA/S Day; **100/101** Powerscourt, AA/M Short; **102** Lough Tay, Wicklow Mountains, AA/C Jones; **111** Cork, AA/S McBride; **112** St Finbarr's Cathedral and South Gate Bridge, AA/C Jones; **113r** Tribute to Rory Gallagher, AA/C Jones; **115** St Anne's Church, K Welsh/Alamy; **116** Bridge in Cork, AA/J Blandford; **117** St Patrick's Street, AA/J Blandford; **118t** Bantry Bay, AA/J Blandford; **118b** Garinish Island, AA/J Blandford; **119** Blarney Castle, AA/S McBride; **120/121** Rock of Cashel, AA/S McBride; **122l** Ring of Kerry, AA/J Blandford; **122/123** Jaunting car, Gap of Dunloe, AA/S McBride; **123r** Killarney, AA/J Blandford; **124/125** Killarney National Park, AA/S McBride; **126t** Kinsale, AA/D Forss; **126c** Kinsale, AA/S McBride; **127** Limerick, AA/P Zollier; **128** Christ Church Cathedral Precinct, AA/M Short; **137** The Burren, AA/S McBride; **138** Cathedral of St Nicholas and Our Lady Assumed into Heaven, AA/C Hill; **140** Eyre Square Arts Festival, AA/L Blake; **141** Statue of Padraic O Conaire, Eyre Square, AA/S McBride; **142** Bunratty Castle, AA/P Zollier; **143** The Burren, AA/S McBride; **144/145** Connemara National Park, AA/C Hill; **145br** Aughanure Castle, AA/C Jones; **146bl** Roundstone harbour, AA/L Blake; **147** Clifden, AA/L Blake; **148/149** Kylemore Abbey, AA/L Blake; **149br** King John's Castle, Athlone, AA/L Blake; **150t** Sligo, AA/J Dawson; **150/151b** Westport House, AA/L Blake; **151r** Thoor Ballylee, AA/S McBride; **159** Royal Opera House, Belfast, AA/J Dawson; **160** Crown Liquor Saloon, Belfast, AA/C Coe; **161** Palm House, Botanic Gardens, AA/G Munday; **162t** City Hall, AA/J Dawson; **162b** Crown Liquor Saloon, AA/G Munday; **163** Laganside, AA/Chris Coe; **164** Ulster Museum, AA; **165t** Grand Opera House, AA/G Munday; **166** Palace stables, Armagh, AA/J Dawson; **167b** Fair Head from Ballycastle Bay, AA/M Diggin; **168** Carrickfergus Castle, AA/D Forss; **169** Pottery wheel at Donegal Craft Village, AA/C Hill; **171** Dunluce Castle, AA/C Coe; **172t** Waterfall in Glenariff, AA/C Coe; **173c** Peace statue, Londonderry, AA/C Coe; **174/175** Carrick-a-Rede Rope Bridge, AA/G Munday; **176** Lough Neagh, AA/G Munday; **177** Tollymore Forest Park, AA; **178** Mount Stewart, AA/G Munday.

Every effort has been made to trace the copyright holders, and we apologise in advance for any accidental errors. We would be happy to apply the corrections in the following edition of this publication.

# Questionnaire

Dear Traveler

Your comments, opinions and recommendations are very important to us. So please help us to improve our travel guides by taking a few minutes to complete this simple questionnaire.

**Send to:** Essential Guides, MailStop 64, 1000 AAA Drive, Heathrow, FL 32746–5063

---

Your recommendations...

We always encourage readers' recommendations for restaurants, nightlife or shopping – if your recommendation is added to the next edition of the guide, we will send you a FREE AAA Essential Guide of your choice. Please state below the establishment name, location and your reasons for recommending it.

_____

_____

_____

_____

_____

Please send me AAA Essential _____

---

About this guide...

Which title did you buy?

_____ **AAA Essential**

Where did you buy it? _____

When? m m / y y

Why did you choose a AAA Essential Guide? _____

_____

_____

_____

Did this guide meet with your expectations?

Exceeded ☐   Met all ☐   Met most ☐   Fell below ☐

Please give your reasons _____

_____

_____

_____

continued on next page...

Were there any aspects of this guide that you particularly liked? _____

_____

_____

_____

_____

Is there anything we could have done better? _____

_____

_____

_____

_____

_____

---

About you...

Name (Mr/Mrs/Ms) _____

Address _____

_____ Zip _____

Daytime tel nos. _____

Which age group are you in?

Under 25 ☐  25–34 ☐  35–44 ☐  45–54 ☐  55–64 ☐  65+ ☐

How many trips do you make a year?

Less than one ☐  One ☐  Two ☐  Three or more ☐

Are you a AAA member?  Yes ☐  No ☐

Name of AAA club _____

---

About your trip

When did you book? m m / y y    When did you travel? m m / y y

How long did you stay? _____

Was it for business or leisure? _____

Did you buy any other travel guides for your trip?  Yes ☐  No ☐

If yes, which ones? _____

_____

Thank you for taking the time to complete this questionnaire.